THE NOVEL LIFE OF
PG WODEHOUSE

Roderick Easdale

ACORN BOOKS
www.acornbooks.co.uk

This edition published in 2014 by
Acorn Books
www.acornbooks.co.uk

Acorn Books is an imprint of
Andrews UK Limited
www.andrewsuk.com

Contents

THE NOVEL LIFE OF PG WODEHOUSE

Traitor?

During the Second World War PG Wodehouse broadcast over the German radio. This bald fact came to dominate everything to do with the man and his works. It skewed appreciation and understanding of his works and cast a cloud over the rest of his life.

For broadcasting on enemy radio, albeit that his talks were intended for neutral America, Wodehouse was denounced as a traitor, a quisling, a fascist, a simpleton, a poor writer, weak-willed, selfish - it seems anything that could be chucked at him in those feverish times was. Few of his detractors had actually heard the broadcasts. But that did not matter. Indeed, ignorance on a subject often serves to clarify someone's views upon it. The man put up to demolish Wodehouse's character on BBC radio had not heard the broadcasts. But this did not prevent - in fact, it probably facilitated - his vituperative decimation of Wodehouse's character on the wireless. Nor did this attack prevent him from becoming good friends with Wodehouse a few years after the end of the war.

Wodehouse was reviled, both during the war and after. Critics confused the man and the message, and judged the work by the worker, some pronouncing him No Longer Funny. His work was deemed by others to be, to use a modern term, politically incorrect. In this, his critics showed as little understanding of his works as they did of the man and the circumstances which lead him to make his broadcasts. One such critic was George Mikes, who wrote in *Eight Humorists*, published in 1954:

> Mr PG Wodehouse is the court jester to the upper classes. He is often irreverent - this is the privilege of court jesters - but there is no doubt about his basic loyalties and, at the bottom of his heart, he is always full of admiration for his titled fools... Mr Wodehouse is supposed to be a critic of, or at least, a caricaturist of the upper classes but, in fact, he is their sycophant, just like the gossip-writers in the evening papers... His childish snobbishness, however, is always out there and always irritating. He accepts the position of 'our betters' in society. Jeeves is a feudal figure - one of the greatest virtues being his fidelity.

In his analysis, Mikes makes error upon error. He misunderstands Jeeves' motives - and thus cannot grasp a lot of the comedy in the Jeeves stories - and in claiming that Wodehouse is 'always full of admiration for his titled fools' he misses the point. But in doing this, Mikes is not alone. There is a strain of opinion that holds that because Wodehouse wrote of the upper classes he must be on their side. By which logic, detective story writers writing about murderers are on the side of the killers.

Lord Emsworth is Wodehouse's most redoubtable figure from the aristocracy, appearing in eleven novels and several short stories. Lord Emsworth has mutated over the course of these chronicles into a sort of hero. Perhaps this is out of readers' sympathy for him, bullied as he is by the female members of his family. Maybe, too, Wodehouse softened his views towards this character as he got older. Indeed, later in life, Wodehouse liked to identify himself with this bumbling old man put upon by female relatives (as with much to do with Wodehouse, it would be unwise to take this at face value). But the portrayal of Lord Emsworth is not all that sympathetic. In the novels, he is normally one of the supporting cast; it is in the short stories that he is more often given a starring role. The first of these to be published was *The Custody Of The Pumpkin* in the *Saturday Evening Post*, and then *The Strand*, in 1924. Lord Emsworth sacks his head gardener over an argument as to whether his niece can stay with him and 'No tinge of remorse did he feel at the thought that Angus McAllister had served him faithfully for ten years. Nor did it cross his mind that he might miss McAllister.'

The sub-plot of this short story concerns Freddie's engagement. When Lord Emsworth learns that his younger son Freddie - and 'practically any behaviour on the part of his son Frederick had the power to irritate him' - is to marry and move abroad, he is puzzled as he 'could conceive of no way in which Freddie could be of value to a dog-biscuit firm, except possibly as a taster', but above all, he is delighted: 'The getting rid of Freddie, which he himself had been unable to achieve in twenty-six years, this godlike dog-biscuit manufacturer had accomplished in less than a week.'

In *The Custody Of The Pumpkin*, Lord Emsworth, as a representative of the British aristocracy, is painted in an unflattering light. Over the course of the books the social critique lessens, but he is never an admirable figure. He is weak, cares little for anyone else and evades his responsibilities. Of these characteristics, the second is the more damning. Asked whether his pig matters more to him than his son, he is surprised at the question: obviously the pig is more important. We, the outsiders, can laugh - but would we want a father like that?

> 'Unlike the male codfish, which, suddenly finding itself the parent of three million five hundred thousand little codfish, cheerfully resolves to love them all, the British aristocracy is apt to look with a somewhat jaundiced eye on its younger sons.' [*The Custody Of The Pumpkin*]

The Custody of the Pumpkin was collected into *Blandings Castle And Elsewhere*, as the opening story. The second story in this collection is *Lord Emsworth Acts For The Best*. In this his butler, Beach, decides to tender his resignation because Lord Emsworth has grown a beard:

> 'That beard is weakening his lordship's position throughout the entire countryside. Are you aware that at the recent Sunday school treat I heard cries of 'Beaver'?'
> 'No.'
> 'Yes! And the spirit of mockery and disrespect will spread. And, what is more, that beard is alienating the best elements in the County.'

It is one of the aspects of Wodehouse's world that the aristocracy is supported from below. It is the butler, not the lord, who cares about his lordship's place in society. It is Jeeves who is more alive to what is proper in Bertie Wooster's attire than the wearer. In *Something Fresh*, the servants are shown to be more concerned with subtle divisions in rank and status than those above stairs. Beach looks down upon the lower classes and deplores that 'the modern tendency of the Lower Classes to get above themselves is becoming more marked every day.' When Bertie's valet, then going under the name Brinkley, tries to murder him in a drunken rage he still dutifully calls him 'Sir'.

When, in *Lord Emsworth And The Girl Friend*, an emboldened Lord Emsworth defeats McAllister in argument and suggests that if he is not happy then he could tender his resignation,

> It had never occurred to him that his employer would voluntarily suggest that he sought another position, and now that he had suggested it, Angus McAllister

disliked the idea very much. Blandings Castle was in his bones. Elsewhere, he would feel in exile.

Another of the themes in Wodehouse's fiction is how the aristocracy themselves are trapped by their social position. Lord Emsworth has no real desire to be in the situation he is. He wants no responsibility to the neighbourhood, no role in one of Britain's two legislative assemblies, and is only ever recorded as attending Parliament for the ceremonial opening, never of actually voting in it. His role in society, through an accident of birth, obliges him to have responsibilities he does not care for. One can either criticise him for having no sense of civic duty, or sympathise with him for his accident of birth. Would Lord Emsworth not be happier living the simpler life of a pigman-cum-gardener? In some of the later Wodehouse works, though not in the Blandings series, the aristocracy are seen as being literally imprisoned in their grand houses. They do not want them, finding them too expensive to keep up and uncomfortable to live in, but they are forced to remain there unless they can offload to a buyer wanting to buy into an empty dream, or a dream which can only be realised through the injection of money from the New World.

> Willoughby, the younger son, who after the fashion of younger sons had been thrust out into the world to earn his living, was now in the highest tax bracket: Crispin, the heir, was forced to take in paying guests in order to make both ends meet: and now there was a yawning between them of two hundred and three pounds six shillings and fourpence. [*The Girl In Blue*] 'Who wants a house nowadays that's miles from anywhere and about the size of Buckingham Palace? And look at the way it eats up money. Repairs, repairs, everlasting repairs - the roof, the stairs, the ceilings, the plumbing, there's no end to it. And that's just inside. Outside, trees need pruning, hedges need

clipping, acres of grass that doesn't cut itself, and the lake smelling to heaven if the weeds aren't cleaned out every second Thursday. And the tenants. Those farmers sit up nights trying to think of new ways for you to spend money on them. It's enough to make a man dotty. I remember, when I was a boy, Father used to take me round the park at Mellingham and say "Some day, Crispin, all this will be yours." He ought to have added "And may the Lord have mercy on your soul".' [*The Girl In Blue*]

In *A Damsel In Distress* Lord Marshmoreton regrets his accession to the peerage, and what it has transformed him into:

'A lot of silly nonsense!' grumbled the earl.
'What is?'
'This foolery of titles and aristocracy. Silly fetish-worship! One man's as good as another...
Damned silly nonsense! When I was a boy I wanted to be an engine driver. When I was a young man, I was a Socialist and hadn't an idea except to work for my living and make a name for myself. I was going to the colonies. Canada. The fruit farm was actually bought. Bought and paid for!' He brooded a moment on that long-lost fruit farm. 'My father was a younger son. And then my uncle must go and break his neck hunting, and the baby, poor little chap, got croup or something... And there I was, saddled with the title, and all my plans gone up in smoke... Silly nonsense! Silly nonsense!' He bit the end of a cigar. 'And you can't stand up against it,' he went on ruefully. 'It saps you. It's like some dammed drug. I fought against it as long as I could, but it is no use. I'm as big a snob as any of them now. I'm afraid to do what I want to do.

Always thinking of the family dignity. I haven't taken a free step for twenty-five years.'

In *A Damsel In Distress*, it is Lady Caroline who is the grande dame determined to thwart young love:

> 'Money,' resumed Lady Caroline, 'is immaterial. Maud is in no position to be obliged to marry a rich man. What makes the thing impossible is that Mr Bevan is nobody. He comes from nowhere. He has no social standing whatsoever.'
> 'Don't see it,' said Lord Marshmoreton. 'The fellow's a thoroughly decent fellow. That's all that matters.'

There is a mistaken view that Wodehouse's work contains no satire. When the book opens, Lady Caroline is going away from the castle for a night so as to give a short talk to the Social Progress League at Lewisham.

Wodehouse always sided with those who challenge snobbishness. If the leading lady of the family forbids a marriage to someone unsuitable, according to her narrow view of what is acceptable - which is inevitably money, breeding, or both - it is guaranteed that they will be overcome. In *Heavy Weather* and *Summer Lightning* the females of the family are opposed to the chorus girl Sue Brown marrying Ronnie Fish. However, as Wodehouse makes clear, it is Sue Brown who is the catch, not Ronnie Fish, nephew of Lord Emsworth. Ronnie is lucky to get her, and probably does not deserve her. Wodehouse makes this clear, too.

You do not have to snarl to insult. That Wodehouse writes with charm and wit and with a smile on his face does not prevent him from putting the boot in on occasion, albeit elegantly and gently. Too much can be made of this. Wodehouse is not a writer principally concerned with a message. He wrote to entertain, to amuse, progressively so. But if one is determined to find a message in his work, it is most definitely not one of uncritical worship of the upper classes.

But Wodehouse's analysis was not prescriptive. If he could be censorious of the inherited political class, he certainly had little time for the elected political class. In *Psmith, Journalist*, Psmith hunts for a particular slum landlord. When he finds his man, it is a Mr Waring, who is standing for alderman in New York. But Psmith is not interested in exposing him, only in getting the tenement improved by Mr Waring as 'it seems to me that it doesn't much matter who gets elected...the other candidates appear to be a pretty fair contingent of blighters.'

In *Uneasy Money*, Wrench the butler, who had previously been in service to Dowager Duchess of Waveney, is now in service to Lady Wetherby, who has a pet monkey, Eustace. We are told:

> He disapproved of Eustace. The Dowager Duchess of Waveney, though she kept open house for members of Parliament, would have drawn the line at monkeys.

Often, as with this example, Wodehouse's comments on politicians are purely abusive. When he justifies his contempt it normally surrounds their hypocrisy. In *Hot Water* the plot revolves around Senator Opal, eminent as a 'dry' senator who had proposed severe legislation in support of this aim, trying to retrieve a letter he wrote to his bootlegger. During the action of the story, the holidaying senator goes to a hotel each afternoon to have a snifter.

In *Jill The Reckless*, Wodehouse paints one of his most unflattering characters in the MP Sir Derek Underhill. Interestingly, the aristocracy are criticised for not taking their positions seriously, but Underhill gets it in the neck for viewing his position too earnestly. Seeking to condemn the MP, Wodehouse gives the words to Freddie Rooke, one of the biggest stage dudes to find his way into Wodehouse's fiction. Underhill decides not to marry Jill, despite having travelled to

New York to reclaim her after he had broken their engagement, because she is in the chorus:

> 'I have to be sensible,' he said chaffing as the indignity of his position intruded more and more. 'You know what it would mean... Paragraphs in all the papers... photographs... the news cabled to England... everybody recording it and misunderstanding... I've got my career to think of... It would cripple me...'
> His voice trailed off, and there was silence for a moment. Then Freddie burst into speech. His good-natured face was hard with unwonted scorn. Its cheerful vacuity had changed to stony contempt. For the second time in the evening the jolly old scales had fallen from Freddie's good old eyes, and, as Jill had done, he saw Derek as he was.
> 'My sainted aunt!' he said slowly. 'So that's it, what? Well I've thought a dashed lot of you, as you know. I've always looked up to you as a bit of a nib and wished I was like you. But, great Scott! If that's the sort of chap you are, I'm dashed glad I'm not! I'm going to wake up in the middle of the night and think how unlike you I am and pat myself on the back! Ronny Devereux was perfectly right. A tick's a tick, and that's all there is to say about it. Good old Ronny told me what you are, and, like a silly ass, I wasted a lot of time trying to make him believe you weren't that sort of chap at all. It's no good standing there like your mother,' said Freddie firmly. 'This is where we jolly well part brass-rags! If we ever meet again, I'll trouble you not to speak to me, for I have got a reputation to keep up!'

But the politician Wodehouse is most famous for having a go at is Roderick Spode, a character based upon Sir Oswald Mosley. Wodehouse would incorporate actual people onto his stories under a loose disguise, such as the preacher Billy Sunday appearing as Jimmy Munday.

Sir Oswald Mosley, once a Conservative supporter, then a Labour MP and minister, set up the British Union of Fascists in 1932. When he did so the *Evening Standard* ridiculed him as 'an obscure member of the disappearing and politically impotent landowning classes.' These are the people Wodehouse made a career in writing about.

Mosley asked Major-General JFC Fuller, formerly chief of staff to the British Tank Corps, to produce a report on the way that the BUF should be reorganised. Part of this report stated: 'Though the wearing of the blackshirt appeals to young people, it must not be overlooked that this is still an old country, very solid, stable and matter of fact. It is still instinctively a feudal country.' This instinctive nature of British society was something Wodehouse also understood, and mined effectively in his plots.

Using again the technique whereby, for impact, the condemnation of a character is given to someone not normally fluent with the spoken word or deep of thought, he gives the words to Bertie Wooster.

> 'The trouble with you, Spode, is that just because you have succeeded in inducing a handful of half-wits to disfigure the London scene by going about in black shorts, you think you're someone. You hear them shouting 'Heil, Spode!' and you imagine that it is the Voice of the People. That is where you make your bloomer. What the Voice of the People is saying is: "Look at that frightful ass Spode swanking about in footer bags! Did you ever in your puff see such a perfect perisher?"' [*The Code Of The Woosters*]

This speech, and the general anti-Spode line of the book, has been seized upon by some defenders of Wodehouse as a sign that the author was anti-Nazi. This would only work were the BUF similar in its aims and philosophy to the Nazis. It was not. The BUF did not seek to seize power - nor, initially even to stand for election - or to govern. Its aim was to provide an organisation which could help with public order. Though the Nazis and the BUF shared similar views on certain things, they were different beasts, and there was no international alliance between them. Criticisms of Mosley cannot be seen as, *de facto*, criticisms of Hitler or of Nazi philosophy, such as it was. As with Nazism, the philosophies of the BUF were not always clearly defined or coherent.

In his published work, the one comment Wodehouse makes about Hitler is a ridiculing of his moustache in *Buried Treasure*. There were said to be anti-Nazi writings of Wodehouse, which were burned by his wife when the town where they were living in France came under risk of capture by the advancing German army.

The best evidence that Wodehouse was not a Nazi - apart from the little matter that there is no evidence which has been produced to prove that he was - is the way in which he was initially used by the German propaganda machine. The kudos which the Germans had originally sought to gain from Wodehouse's early release from the internment camp was based around a loose understanding of his political views. The Germans knew that he was not a Nazi sympathiser. That was the point: Nazis being nice to a fellow Nazi has no propaganda value. That the Nazis were being nice to an elderly and highly respected writer who happened to be a citizen of the country of their enemy and believed to be unsympathetic to the Nazis has propaganda value. (German tactics concerning the propaganda value were to change after he had made the broadcasts as the result of a battle between different parts of the Nazi machine, but this had been the original plan.)

What is clearly the case is that Wodehouse was not anti-German. With distinctions blurred by war, when many felt it necessary to hate the whole population of the enemy's country, this did not endear him to many Brits. But not all Germans were Nazis, far from it. The Wodehouses had German friends from their time in Hollywood, and after Wodehouse was released he was still initially required to remain within German borders. One of these German friends, Baron von Barnekow, arranged that they could stay with a cousin of his. The Baron was a fervent critic of the Nazis and was shortly to take his own life in desperation at Nazi domination.

That Wodehouse was captured by the Germans has its roots in international taxation law, British quarantine laws, and a desire to show faith in the British forces.

As international taxation laws were still in a relatively primitive state, Wodehouse had run into complications through working extensively in both America and Britain. Put simply, he was at risk of having to pay two loads of tax on the same money. This problem he resolved by moving to France and paying British tax on money he earned in Britain, and American tax on money earned in that country. In 1934 the Wodehouses set up home in Le Touquet, where there were many other ex-pats living.

When the threat of a German invasion began to be taken seriously some of these ex-pats left. The Wodehouses remained. Partly this was from a dislike of having to place their peke Wonder in quarantine for six months should they move to England, but another factor was their desire to show faith in the British forces in the area by not scarpering unless it was really necessary. The Wodehouses were prominent figures in the local community, Plum by virtue of his renown as a writer, Ethel through her enthusiastic party-giving. She saw a role for herself in maintaining morale by entertaining the British forces - the Wodehouses also had billeted at their house two French military doctors. The Wodehouses, like others, were in contact with the British vice-consul in Boulogne and expected to be alerted by him if it became no longer safe to remain in residence. This warning was never given. As with others who had continued to live in the area, it seems that the Wodehouses did not really appreciate the extent of the danger they were in by staying on.

On 21 May the Wodehouses set out in a car chock-full of possessions from their house in Le Touquet. After covering only a short distance, the car broke down having been poorly repaired after a crash some weeks before. This had not previously come to light as they had been using their other car since then. The Wodehouses set out again, this time in convoy with neighbours who were travelling in a van and a car. The van broke down. By the time it was repaired, it was evening and the party decided to return to Le Touquet. That night the Germans captured the town.

Wodehouse was required to report to the German authorities at the nearby town of Paris Plage each day; his wife was required to report once a week. The Germans, working on the principle of 'what's yours is mine', commandeered the Wodehouses' bathroom. This fact, and Wodehouse's comments on it, was to spawn various stories 'proving' Wodehouse's support and sympathies for the Germans. In the first of his broadcasts, Wodehouse made facetious comments about parties of Germans dropping in for a bath at his house. These Germans were as unwelcome as those who raided the Wodehouse's larder and also took away - 'pinched' as Wodehouse said in his first broadcast - their cars, bicycles and radio, and Wodehouse's tobacco. However the Wodehouses were in no position to dictate terms. Wodehouse's sloppily expressed comments became translated down the line into Wodehouse throwing parties for the Germans and inviting them to use his bath. This in turn snowballed into a story about Wodehouse throwing a cocktail party to welcome the Germans.

Two months after the Germans had captured Le Touquet, Wodehouse was interned along with the other foreign males living there. He was taken first to a prison at Loos where, with two friends, he was locked in a cell measuring twelve feet by eight feet for 23½ hours a day. After four days of this treatment the internees complained to the German Camp Kommandant. Having previously had no idea of how the internees were being treated by the French guards, he ordered that the prisoners be allowed to roam about the prison during the day, although they were still to be locked up at night.

Prisoners over 60 years of age were released, and the others were shipped off on a 19-hour journey to Liege, where Wodehouse, just under three months short of his 59th birthday, stayed for a week in an abandoned army barracks. From here the internees were moved on to the mediaeval stone fortress in Huy, where Wodehouse stayed for six weeks, sleeping at night on a thin bedding of straw laid over cobblestones, before being transported by train to a former mental asylum in Tost in Upper Silesia. Whereas for the six-hour journey to Huy the internees were transported in cattle trucks, this one was made in standard passenger carriages. Before the journey each of them was given a sausage and half a loaf of bread. Thirty-two hours later they were given another half loaf and some soup. This was their sole nourishment for a three-and-a-half day journey.

On the journey to Huy Wodehouse had been sustained by another internee, Bert Haskins, who shared with him his personal reserve of food and beer. The two became friends and, after the war, Wodehouse ensured that his publisher sent Haskins a copy of each new book of his. Wodehouse also paid for him to have an annual holiday. In return, Haskins supplied Wodehouse with publications from Britain.

Wodehouse recorded in the notebook he kept during internment that Haskins had been 'extraordinary kind' on the train to Huy. This notebook, which had originally been kept with the aim of producing a book of his experiences, were jottings of his thoughts, together with a few details of events as an *aide memoir* to be written up more fully later. Not for Wodehouse was the hating of all Germans simply because they were German. Though dominated by the issue - in both senses - of food ('It's extraordinary how one's whole soul becomes obsessed with food'), they also reveal a man with compassion and an eye for absurdity. Many of his notes poke fun at the Germans' lack of organisational ability and at his captor's pomposity and petty orders; but others show an understanding that there was a difference between authority and those caught up in the machine. Wodehouse's novels frequently send up authority; so too did his camp notebook. The novelist was the diarist.

Though he found the camp authorities frequently absurd in their pronouncements and incompetence, and was later to ridicule them on radio, he could at the same time write of 'our dear old sergeant' who was to sit an examination to become a lieutenant, and express the hope that he passed. Presumably this is the sergeant who at parade 'announces that he is going home on leave for a few days and is loudly cheered, as we like him enormously.'

Privation and discomfort are recorded matter-of-factly. The idiocies of the situation - or rather, of German authority - are celebrated. When I first read detailed extracts of his camp notebook I found it a strangely touching document. It is the work of a man determined not to whine, to look at the best side of any situation. It is of a man resolved to keep his spirits up, rather than one who was actually enjoying the experience.

This might seem obvious. Would anyone really want to be held prisoner? Well, some commentators have argued that Wodehouse was very contented in camp. They assert that in camp he found a similar atmosphere to that in a public school, and that a man who had been happy at Dulwich College would slide happily into camp life. Though there is undoubtedly at least a grain of truth in Evelyn Waugh's observation that: 'Anyone who has been to an English public school will always feel comparatively at home in prison. It is the people brought up in the gay intimacy of the slums who find prison so soul-destroying,' [*Decline And Fall*] I feel this sentiment can be taken too far. Reading Wodehouse's camp notebook certainly brought to mind recollections from my own public schooldays, mainly of the petty, seemingly pointless rules which were often self-defeating and inconsistently applied. If my housemaster announced that he was leaving us it would have been a matter of rejoicing, but not because we liked him.

Wodehouse was probably easily able to adapt to camp life, but enjoyment is another matter. Those who have argued that he relished it, must, I feel, have been seduced by Wodehouse's determination to make light of it. Wodehouse said towards the end of his final wartime broadcast:

> Life in an internment camp resembles life outside, in that it is what you make it. Nothing can take away the unpleasant feeling of being a prisoner, but you can make an effort and prevent it getting you down. And that it was we did, and what I imagine all the other British prisoners in Germany did.

At Tost, Wodehouse was offered a single room in respect of his age and reputation as a writer. He declined. However the camp authorities hired for him a typewriter - and passed the cost on to him - and provided him with a room where he could work. This he apparently shared with a saxophonist and a tap-dancer. If all three worked there together - well, the mind boggles. Wodehouse was able to write to his wife, who was still in France, and to Paul Reynolds, his agent in America. Thus he continued his writing career as best he could.

While in camp he was interviewed by an American journalist, and wrote an article entitled 'My War With Germany' for the *Saturday Evening Post*, where his novels and short stories were usually serialised before receiving book publication. This article and his interview alerted Americans to Wodehouse's plight. Many wanted him to be 'sent back home' to America. Wodehouse's close friend and writing collaborator Guy Bolton organised a petition which was handed in at the German Embassy in Washington by William Warren Barbour, a United States senator. Paul Reynolds lobbied for his client's release, as did some German-based American correspondents. Germans, also, were trying to get Wodehouse freed, amongst them Baron Raven von Barnekow, who had devised a plan whereby Wodehouse would be exchanged for a German industrialist stranded in Britain.

The decision to release Wodehouse earlier than his 60th birthday started with an initiative by Dr Paul Schmidt, head of the private office of the German Foreign Minister, Ribbentrop. He saw the release of Wodehouse as a way of keeping American opinion on-side, as the Germans were keen to maintain American neutrality, albeit a somewhat lopsided one. Showing the Nazis to be humane in releasing a distinguished writer from captivity, seemingly because of respect for American opinion, could be a component of this policy. The Gestapo, however, refused to sanction any early discharge for Wodehouse.

Here another Paul Schmidt became involved. He was the head of the Foreign Office department which dealt with the American press and a fan of Wodehouse's work. Having already read 'My War With Germany', he suggested to his namesake that Wodehouse might be interested in broadcasting an account of his wartime experiences written in the same light-hearted tone as his magazine article. This would help to publicise Wodehouse's early release. The Gestapo now dropped their objection.

What seems clear, however, is that Wodehouse was unaware of all this. He was expecting to remain in prison until he was 60 and getting on with his writing. If not happy, he had managed to achieve a degree of comfort and peace. Although he made no deal with the Germans in order to obtain his release, he appears to have been unofficially sounded out about his views. The lager führer at the camp, in a conversation about the hire of the typewriter and remarking how he had enjoyed 'My War With Germany', put to Wodehouse the idea that he should deliver some broadcasts on similar lines for his American readers. Wodehouse expressed pleasure at the notion but, he said to Major Cussen, who was charged with investigating Wodehouse after the liberation of France, this conversation was 'quite casual and made no impression on my mind.'

However, it is likely that the German Foreign Office was now aware that, if Wodehouse were approached after he was released, he would willingly agree to their plan for a series of humorous broadcasts. But he was not approached about broadcasting until after his release. If he were to be, it would spoil the German plan. In the first place, it might make Wodehouse suspicious; secondly it would negate the propaganda victory which was planned. As it was, the Gestapo was to make this point redundant as they changed the nature of the propaganda victory which the Germans sought to gain. Goebbels' ministry saw German interests being better served if Wodehouse was seen as a convert to Nazism. In this belief they misunderstood the nature of Wodehouse's work and reputation. Whether someone who celebrated the absurd was quite the type of standard bearer for Nazism that its advocates would want is questionable.

On the evening of 21 June, Wodehouse was summoned from playing in a knockabout game of cricket and told he was being released. As Wodehouse's 60th birthday was on 15 October, he was being released almost four months early, after 42 weeks at Tost. Wodehouse and another prisoner were taken to Berlin, where the two guards who had accompanied them from Tost had to find them a place to stay. This turned out to be the Adlon hotel, where Wodehouse met Major Plack, a casual acquaintance from his time in Hollywood. It was he who put to Wodehouse the proposal to make some broadcasts. Wodehouse readily agreed. For 30 weeks he had been receiving letters from American readers which he had been forbidden to answer. That this might have been seen as a lack of manners irked him. Throughout his life Wodehouse was punctilious in answering fan mail, and in making a series of broadcasts he saw an opportunity to thank his American correspondents. Also, we can presume, there could have been a professional reason for a journalist and writer wanting to broadcast a series of talks. Wodehouse liked writing, and this was a writing job.

He had delivered some talks about his wartime experiences to his fellow internees at Tost. These had been well received. This, however, was an audience which would have been on his wavelength. They would understand the internees' code of not whining, which underpinned everything he said, and would have experienced the petty rules and regulations and bureaucratic incompetence which so amused Wodehouse. They would also presumably enjoy the way he sent these up; he would have been delivering his talks to people who were in on the joke. This was not the case with his broadcasts for a more general audience. One among these was Air Marshal Boyd, who told his personal assistant, 'Why the Germans ever let him say all this I cannot think. They have either got more sense of humour than I credited them with, or it has just slipped past the censor. There is some stuff about them being packed into cattle trucks and a thing about Loos jail which you would think would send a Hun crazy. Wodehouse has probably been shot by now.' Perhaps crucial to this assessment was that Air Marshall Boyd was himself a prisoner of war. He knew where Wodehouse was coming from, and what he was attempting to do.

Wodehouse recorded five talks to be broadcast by the Germans to America. These were talks he wrote and delivered himself. Here are some extracts typical of their style:

> I don't know who first started the rumour that we were going to the barracks at Liege, but he turned out to be quite right. That was where we were headed for and at eleven o'clock next morning we were given our mid-day soup and hustled out and dumped into vans and driven to our station.
> One would have supposed from the atmosphere of breathless bustle that the train was scheduled to pull out at about eleven-thirty, but this was not the case.

Our Kommandant was a careful man. I think he must have once missed an important train, and it preyed on his mind. At any rate, he got us there at eleven-forty a.m. and the journey actually started at eight o'clock in the evening. I can picture the interview between him and the sergeant when the latter returned. 'Did those boys make the train?... Yes, sir, -by eight hours and twenty minutes'...Whew! Close thing. Mustn't run it so fine another time. [Second broadcast]

The arrangements for our reception at Liege seemed incomplete. It was as if one had got to a party much too early. Here, for instance, were eight hundred men who were going to live mostly on soup - and though the authorities knew where to lay their hand on some soup all right, nothing had been provided to put it in. And eight hundred internees can't just go to the cauldron and lap. For one thing, they would burn their tongues, and another the quick swallowers would get more than their fair share. The situation was one that called for quick thinking, and it was due to our own resourcefulness that this problem was solved. At the back of the barrack yard there was an enormous rubbish heap, into which Belgian soldiers through the ages had been dumping old mess tins, old cans, cups with bits chipped off them, bottles, kettles and containers for motor oil. We dug them out, gave them a wash and a brush up, and there we were. I had the good fortune to secure one of the motor oil containers. It added to the taste of the soup something that the others hadn't got. [Third broadcast]

At Tost we had a noticeboard on which camp orders were posted each day, but this ingenious system had not occurred to anyone at Huy. The only way they could think of there of establishing communication between the front office and the internee was to call a parade. Three whistles would blow, and we would assemble in the yard, and after a long interval devoted to getting into some sort of formation we would be informed that there was a parcel for Omer - or that we must shave daily - or that we must not smoke on parade - or that we must not keep our hands in our pockets on parade - or that we might buy playing cards - (and that next day that we might not buy playing cards) - or that boys must not cluster round the guard room trying to scrounge food from the soldiers - or that there was a parcel for Omer. [Fourth broadcast]

In the penultimate paragraph of the final broadcast - the final one was a 'thank you' to those who had written to him in camp - he spoke of how rumours were important to camp life, and how they were nicknamed 'bedtime stories':

These bedtime stories never turned out to be true, but a rumour a day kept depression away, so they served their purpose. Certainly, whether owing to bedtime stories or simply the feeling, which I myself had, that, if one was in, one was in and it was no use making heavy weather about it, the morale of the men at Tost was wonderful. I never met a more cheerful crowd, and I loved them like brothers.

In America, Wodehouse's words and actions were noted by those in power. Recognising his genius in going on German radio ridiculing his captors and stating how high morale was among those imprisoned, the American War Department made the texts of his broadcasts part of the syllabus at Camp Ritchie as an example of anti-Nazi propaganda.

The British government had spent time and money on producing wartime propaganda ridiculing the Germans. Now they had a wonderful example of the Germans being lampooned by one of the finest comic writers alive. Moreover, on German radio, he had spoken of the high morale of British prisoners. What a stupendously wonderful propaganda opportunity this presented.

So, how did the British government seek to exploit this amazing opportunity? With a display of utter fatheadedness.

Rather than seeking to spread the word of what Wodehouse had said, it poured vitriol on the author. What it hoped to achieve by this is not clear. Whether it was even clear to those who devised and carried out the action has to be questioned. Was it merely an outpouring of fury that a famous British author was broadcasting on German radio? Was it designed to bolster British resolve? It had been suggested that there was anger that Wodehouse was broadcasting to America, whom the British government wanted to enter the war against Germany, and it was afraid that Wodehouse's words might make this less likely. Does one light novelist and farceur have so much power? If so, this was surely a case of barking up the wrong tree, as the political powers in America were forming their own judgement on the broadcasts and their, extremely rational, conclusion was that Wodehouse was not pro-Nazi.

British establishment thinking appears muddled. Or just too narrow-minded. Rather than using some lateral thinking and investigating what Wodehouse had said and seeing how best to utilise it in a positive manner, their reaction seems to be the knee-jerk one of a bully. After a lunch - reported as a boozy one where six were present - Alfred Duff Cooper, Minister of Information, decided that William Connor, a journalist who wrote under the pen name Cassandra, should be put up to give a ten-minute talk on BBC radio attacking Wodehouse. The idea was originally to broadcast this talk to America, to negate whatever damage the government felt Wodehouse's broadcasts to that country had done. Later it was decided to broadcast this attack over the Home Service as well as the Empire Service.

This talk was delivered on 15 July. By this date Wodehouse had made two broadcasts from Berlin, both monitored by the BBC. The governors of the BBC objected to the planned broadcast, telling Duff Cooper that their monitoring of Wodehouse's talks had shown them to be free of any pro-Nazi or anti-British sentiments. Duff Cooper ignored their objection, knowing that, under wartime regulations, the BBC had to provide airtime for government propaganda. The governors responded with their lawyers' opinion that, as the attack on Wodehouse was slanderous, Wodehouse could sue the corporation. Duff Cooper's response was that the Government would bear the costs of any action and damages resulting from the broadcast.

Thus it was that the BBC carried a vituperative attack on PG Wodehouse, its force made stronger by the fact that it came directly after the reportage of the nine o'clock news. The following are extracts from this talk:

I have come to tell you tonight of the story of a rich man trying to seek his last and greatest sale - that of his own country. It is a sombre story of self-respect, of honour and decency being pawned to the Nazis for the price of a soft bed in a luxury hotel... When war broke out Wodehouse was at Le Touquet - gambling. Nine months later he was still there. Poland had been wiped out. Denmark had been overrun and Norway had been occupied. Wodehouse went on with his fun. The elderly playboy didn't believe in politics. He said so. No good time Charlie ever does. Wodehouse was throwing a cocktail party when the storm troopers clumped in on his shallow life...

Wodehouse was steadily being groomed for stardom, the most disreputable stardom in the world - the limelight of quislings. On the last day of June this year, Dr Goebbels was ready. So too was Pelham Wodehouse. He was eager and he was willing and when they offered him Liberty in a country which has killed Liberty, he leapt at it. And Dr Goebbels, taking him high into the mountain, showed him all the Kingdoms of the world...and said unto him: 'All this power will I give you if you worship the Führer.' Pelham Wodehouse fell on his knees...

Fifty thousand of our countrymen are enslaved in Germany.... they endure but they do not give in. They suffer but do not sell out.

The talk continued in this vein. Cassandra, who in his talk accused Wodehouse of tax evasion, was paid 20 guineas. It is a shocking piece of journalism. Cassandra had pitched his talk for maximum effect, and in this he succeeded.

Opinion in Britain was swung against Wodehouse. To some patriotism equalled hating Wodehouse. His books, once taken from library shelves to be borrowed, were now taken off them to be suppressed. It was open season on Wodehouse, though many urged restraint until the facts of the case became known, and others condemned Cassandra's antics as strongly as others were condemning the behaviour in which they believed Wodehouse to have indulged.

Some who attacked Wodehouse merely did so through genuine, though misguided, feelings of patriotism. Others saw it as a chance to attack a literary reputation they considered undeserved, and in particular his award of an honorary degree from Oxford University. Sean O'Casey wrote, in a letter to the press, that:

It is amusing to read the various wails about the villainy of Wodehouse. The harm done to England's cause and to England's dignity is not the poor man's babble in Berlin, but the acceptance of him by a childish part of the people and the academic government of Oxford, dead from the chin up, as a person of any importance whatsoever in English humorous literature, or any literature at all. [*The Daily Telegraph*, 3 July, 1941]

EC Bentley also wrote to the national press:

There is only one opinion about Mr PG Wodehouse's bargain with the German Government; but those who feel it most keenly on the subject, I should imagine, are the learned body responsible for conferring upon him the Oxford Doctorate of Letters in 1939.

Oxford in recent years has been suffering from an attack of what may be called the 'Why-Shouldn't-I's'; and the most distressing symptom of it was the bestowal of one of the highest literary distinctions in the world upon one who has never written a serious line.

Amends can be made, however. Those who awarded the honour can take the earliest opportunity of removing it. This action would have a certain effectiveness, not only as a mark of disapproval but as a sign of repentance; and most of my fellow-graduates, I believe, would heartily welcome it on both grounds.' [*The Daily Telegraph*, 8 July, 1941]

Others saw an opportunity to use Wodehouse's broadcasts to make political points of their own. The Communist newspaper the *Daily Worker* opined that:

We do not dispute that Wodehouse is as petty and contemptible as the ruling-class characters portrayed in his bestsellers. But since when has amiability and boneheadedness been an excuse for serving Goebbels?

The sloppy Wodehouse broadcasts from Berlin were deliberately selected by the subtle German propagandists. Better a famous British author expressing doubts about the victory of his own country than a second Haw-Haw churning out fantastic lies.

Wodehouse represents the rottenness that infected a section of Britain in the years preceding the war. His day is over.

Wodehouse, when he became aware of how English public opinion - albeit manufactured - viewed his broadcasts, was horrified. Thrice he appealed to the Germans to be allowed to return to England to explain and defend himself: a naive request.

It was not just the five scripted talks which Wodehouse broadcast which had caused a storm. On his discharge, Wodehouse had been interviewed by Harry W. Flannery, the American correspondent in Berlin of the Columbia Broadcasting System, on 26 June. Flannery perceived a chance to attack Nazism by making Wodehouse look a foolish traitor, which is what he genuinely thought he was. As was customary at that time, the interview was scripted and read out by the participants. Flannery wrote the script, and in doing so deliberately tried to show Wodehouse in a poor light. Wodehouse walked into the trap, naively reading out Flannery's responses:

Flannery: Do you mind being a prisoner of war in this fashion?
Wodehouse: Not a bit. As long as I have a typewriter and plenty of paper and a room to work in, I'm fine.

Later Wodehouse read from Flannery's script:

I'm wondering whether the kind of people and the kind of England I write about, will live after the war - whether England wins or not, I mean.

The first comment Wodehouse thought would demonstrate a cheerful British stiff-upper-lip attitude, a determination to make the best of a bad job. This was the code of the internee, and Wodehouse viewed his comments through these eyes. To the outsider, it could appear that he was living in high luxury, swanning about in German high society. The comments about England winning or not just seem to have slipped past the radar of a too-trusting Wodehouse. In a 1946 interview with Hubert Cole of *Illustrated* he explained the comments:

> Cole: The phrase which has been singled out in your talks as being defeatist and pro-Nazi is 'whether England wins or not'. Why did you include this in your script?
> Wodehouse: I didn't. There is no such phrase in my talks. It occurred in a brief interview with me by the American representative of the Columbia Broadcasting System in Berlin. He wrote the entire script, including the words you mention, and I read them out without realising their intention. I did not even notice them at the time.

After the three-and-a-half minute interview with Flannery, listeners had been returned to the New York studio, where the presenter Elmer Davis said:

> Mr Wodehouse's many friends in the United States will be glad to know that he is free and that he is apparently comfortable and happy. Mr Wodehouse seems to be more fortunate than most of the other Englishmen in his internment camp, whose release would perhaps have less publicity value for the Germans, and, of course, he was only in an internment camp to begin with, which is very different from a concentration camp. People who get out of concentration camps, such as Dachau, for

instance - well, in the first place, not a great many of them get out, and, when they do, they are seldom able to broadcast.

Wodehouse had been well and truly stitched up. The words of the interview became mixed up in public minds, and public prints, with his broadcasts, and the rumour mill further jumbled everything up and added to it so that Wodehouse was said to have said and done all sorts of things which he had not.

Major Plack, who was charged with the supervision of the Wodehouses, was diligent in ensuring their comfort and peace of mind as far as was possible. The Wodehouses had to pay their way in Germany. In the winter months they stayed at the Adlon hotel - the German authorities' choice not theirs. In the summer they stayed with friends in the country, until accommodation in Berlin became scarcer as Berlin was increasingly flattened and led to the Wodehouses being despatched to Paris. They were able to pay their way only because Ethel Wodehouse sold some of her jewellery and from some continuing payments from Wodehouse's writing. Even then they had to rely upon loans from friends to make up the deficit. Wodehouse was able to receive some royalties from his book sales - which were channelled through the German authorities, leading to some confusion and stories that he 'had been paid by the Germans' - and he sold a short story to a Paris newspaper and the film rights of one of his novels to a German company. As part of the sale came the stipulation that the film was not made until after the war and no publicity was to be given to the transaction lest it be used for propaganda purposes.

After France was liberated, Major Cussen rapidly came to the conclusion that Wodehouse was not guilty of treachery. Of necessity, with the war still continuing and German records unavailable to him, his inquiry could only be partial. He concluded, however, in his report on the matter of Wodehouse's wartime behaviour that:

It seems clear that the actual text of the Wodehouse broadcasts does not contain material of a pro-German character, and the view may well be taken that the mere words used by Wodehouse in his broadcasts were unlikely to assist the enemy.

Upon the information at present available it seems, subject always to the decision of the Director of Public Prosecutions, that Wodehouse has not been guilty of treasonable conduct and his conduct does not bring him within the terms of Section 1 of the Treachery Act 1940.

'That Wodehouse is not a traitor as far as we know, but he might be' is a fair summary of British government policy over Wodehouse. He was never totally cleared, although a knighthood conferred days before he died at a great age was seen by many as a sign of acceptance that he had not behaved dishonourably. In the absence of this official clearance rumours were allowed to ferment. The BBC attack on Wodehouse had struck home, especially as they continued to ban his works for some years after the war was over. Years later the 'facts' of Cassandra's talk were still trotted out by reviewers as the 'truth' of Wodehouse's wartime activities.

In 1947 when Wodehouse left France, it was for America, where he was sure that he would remain a free man even though press opinion in America had also been hostile to him. *The New York Times*, for example, had written in September 1942 that he had 'accepted German hospitality on a luxurious scale'; the next year it said he had 'been installed at the Adlon hotel at the expense of the German government' and in July 1944 it reflected on the fact that he 'had broadcast from Berlin advocating a separate peace'.

Unsure whether he might be arrested if he were to return to his homeland, he never did. The last 36 years of his life were spent, effectively, in exile. When Iain Sproat finally achieved the release of official papers on Wodehouse's wartime conduct, they declared no guilt on Wodehouse. Yet the impression that Wodehouse was guilty had been left to remain rooted in the public mind through government secrecy. Those who favour the 'cock-up' theory of history can see this as just another example. Conspiracy theorists can divine a reluctance by government to admit to error, especially as it could, at least in theory, lead to the defence of a large libel action. I prefer the cock-up theory - here caused by natural inertia and ignorance combined with a culture of secrecy. In truth it is hard to point to such a thing as 'The Government'; what there is is a disjointed, amorphous body made of conflicting interests, transitory people and changing policies.

It has to be considered whether Wodehouse, far from being too dim to understand the implications of his broadcasts, was too clever. His broadcasts were clever and subtle, too much so for the manufactured force of a public opinion which was hampered by limited imagination and information. Had the British government shared Wodehouse's intelligence and imagination then this particular bit of wartime history could have been very different.

Many have defended Wodehouse's actions during the war by asserting that he was unworldly, an author all at sea outside the confines of his writing, lacking a full understanding of life and human nature. In his excellent *PG Wodehouse: Man And Myth*, Barry Phelps spends a lot of time demonstrating that Wodehouse was far more astute than he let on. Even if one allows the argument that Wodehouse the writer was a genius, but Wodehouse the private man was a bit of a naive simpleton, it was Wodehouse the writer who wrote, in 1910, in *Psmith In The City* about the unloved bank manager's successful campaign for parliament:

> It had been discovered, on the eve of the poll, that the bank manager's opponent, in his youth, had been educated at a school in Germany, and had subsequently spent two years at Heidelberg

University. These damaging revelations were having a marked effect on the warm-hearted patriots of Kenningford, who were now referring to the candidate in thick but earnest tones as 'The German Spy'.

Where was the man who wrote these words when he was needed 30 years later? Wodehouse had it in him to foresee how his actions would be misunderstood. But, in his eagerness to thank his American correspondents, he forget the wider picture. It cost him dear.

Upbringing

Wodehouse was brought up by a series of aunts. This has been used to explain why so many aunts, and so few parents, appear in his work. Particularly, it has been used to explain why the heavies in the Wooster stories are invariably aunts: Wodehouse was getting his own back on those who had made his early years a misery. After all, he would not be the first such writer to do so, runs the argument, with others such as Kipling and Saki being positioned in the same stable. This is too simplistic a view.

The Wodehouses were of the landed gentry and of the aristocracy. The Wodehouse family had risen to the latter when Sir John Wodehouse MP was created Baron Wodehouse of Kimberley in 1797. He was PG Wodehouse's great-great uncle. The third baron, Wodehouse's third cousin, was made Earl of Kimberley in 1866. Wodehouse's great-great grandfather was a baronet. Many of the aristocrats in Wodehouse's fiction came unexpectedly to their titles by circuitous routes snaking through the family tree. One such is the third Earl of Havershot:

> When I say that I'm the third Earl of Havershot, I don't mean that I was always that... But you know how it is. Uncles call it a day. Cousins hand in their spades and buckets. And little by little and bit by bit, before you know where you are - why there you are, don't you know. [*Laughing Gas*]

Philip Wodehouse was knighted on the battlefield by the Earl of Essex for his valour at the Battle of Cadiz in 1596, and in 1611 he bought his baronetcy from King James VI of Scotland and I of England. The fifth baronet, Sir Armine Wodehouse, had two sons. The younger, Revd Philip Wodehouse was father to Colonel Philip Wodehouse who, aged 27, fought at the Battle of Waterloo. Aged 43, the Colonel married. The youngest of his five children was Henry Ernest (although he was to be known always as Ernest), born in July 1845. A year and half later the Colonel died. Ernest Wodehouse was to grow up not knowing his father. Neither, in turn, were the oldest three of Ernest's four sons, of whom PG Wodehouse was the third, to know their father while they were growing up. But not, in this case, through death, but geography.

PG Wodehouse was a scion of an ancient Norfolk family. The Norfolk branch of the Wodehouse family can be traced back to 1402, the year that John Wodehouse was made Constable of Castle Rising. As major landowners, the Wodehouses were of the political class. Through the centuries Wodehouses were returned to the House of Commons, notably Sir John Wodehouse, who entered government in 1852 as Under-Secretary of State for Foreign Affairs and left it in 1895 as Secretary of State for Foreign Affairs, by which time he was the Earl of Kimberley.

Those Wodehouses who did not interest themselves in politics often went into the church. It was the local landowner who appointed the parish priest. At around the time of PG Wodehouse's birth the Kimberley estates ran to more than 10,000 acres of Norfolk, as well as a few hundred acres in Cornwall. With the landholding came the advowson of eleven parishes. This right to appoint the parish priest - although in Lord Emsworth's case it is perhaps better described as a chore - is a plot line Wodehouse uses with both Lord Emsworth and Sir Watkyn Bassett possessing the right of advowson.

Four of Wodehouse's fifteen uncles were clergymen. Wodehouse himself was not particularly religious. Although he attended church services in camp, this appears to be the exception rather than the rule in his case. Late in life, Wodehouse described himself as an agnostic. While he was contemptuous of politicians in his writing, the other family profession, as it were, comes across as an honourable occupation. His clergy are decent men, but not noticeably devout or religious. The job of a clergyman for them veers more towards being an occupation rather than a calling, one of practicality rather than spirituality. This, one suspects, was the case with many of the clergy created from the younger sons and nephews of the landed gentry, set up in a parish with a stipend and a church house.

Ernest Wodehouse had joined the civil service in Hong Kong after being educated at Repton. In Hong Kong he had met Eleanor, who was visiting her brother, who was also in the civil service out there. They were married on 3 February 1877. Any children of theirs were going to be assured of having many aunts: Eleanor was the fifth of fourteen children of her clergyman father, the Revd John Bathurst Deane, who had been born in the Cape of Good Hope, the son of Captain Charles Meredith Deane of the 24th Light Dragoons. He went to the Merchant Taylors' School and Pembroke College, Cambridge, before taking holy orders. He was the author of four books on religious or military matters. One was a biography of a relative, *The Life of Richard Deane, Major General and General at Sea in the Service of the Commonwealth*; another was entitled *The Worship of the Serpent, Traced Throughout the World and its Traditions Referred to in the Events in Paradise Proving The Temptation and Fall of Man.*

'He writes books?'
'He has written one. He calls it Hypnotism As A Device To Uncover The Unconscious Drives And Mechanisms In An Effort To Analyse The Functions Involved Which Give Rise To Emotional Conflicts In The Waking State but the title's going to be changed

to Sleepy Time. Popgood thinks it's snappier.' [*Sleepy Time*]

On 26 September - an uncomfortably short time since their wedding - Ernest and Eleanor Wodehouse had their first son. He was the first English child to be born on the Peak, an exclusive residential area of Hong Kong, and was christened Philip Peveril. Philip was a name long popular in the family, Peveril came from Sir Walter Scott's *Peveril Of The Peak*. Peveril was the name by which he came to be known. Their second child was born in England on 11 May 1879 and christened Ernest Armine; Ernest after his father and Armine because, like Philip, it was a popular Christian name for Wodehouses through the generations. He, too, was known by his second name.

People give their children all sorts of rummy names. [*Indiscretions of Archie*]

PG Wodehouse was born on 15 October 1881 at 1 Vale Place, 50 Epsom Road in Guildford in Surrey, the third son to Eleanor and Ernest Wodehouse. The address was that of one of his aunts, on his mother's side. Eleanor Wodehouse was on an extended visit from Hong Kong. PG Wodehouse started life in an aunt's house, and he was to spend much of his youth in one. He was christened Pelham Grenville in honour of the man who was to become his godfather, Colonel von Donop.

'His name's not Lemuel?'
'I fear so, sir.'
'Couldn't he use his second name?'
'His second name is Gengulphus.'
'Golly, Jeeves,' I said thinking of old Uncle Tom Portarlington, 'there's some raw work pulled at the font from time to time, is there not?' [*Jeeves And The Feudal Spirit*]

If you surmised from the fact that he presented himself to the world as 'PG Wodehouse' that Pelham Grenville Wodehouse did not like his Christian names, you would be correct. To family and friends he was known as 'Plum' or, more rarely, 'Plummie'. Eleven years after son number three came a fourth and final one, Richard Lancelot, known as Dick.

Wodehouse's grandfather was not the only author on the mother's side of the family. Wodehouse's Aunt Mary was a professional writer who published twelve books, the most successful of which was a historical romance set in eighteenth-century Bath. A fearsome lady, Mary is credited with being the basis of Bertie Wooster's Aunt Agatha. Louisa, as the oldest of Revd Deane's children, was lumbered with the task of being a surrogate parent. Much liked by Wodehouse, she became the inspiration for Aunt Dahlia, Bertie's slightly dubiously titled 'good' aunt. A more accurate description would be that she was the aunt whom Bertie liked.

When Revd Deane died in 1887 at Sion Hill, Bath, his widow and the four unmarried daughters moved to a house in Box. Here Wodehouse was to spend much of his childhood, and when he was at Dulwich College this was listed as his home address during the period that his parents were still resident in Hong Kong. The set up is recreated in *The Mating Season*, written two years after the final one of the aunts, Emmeline, an artist, died. The house in the novel is given as Deverill Court - there were five villages near his aunts' house named Brixton Deverill, Monkton Deverill, Kingston Deverill, Longbridge Deverill and Hill Deverill.

But how far does the aunt connection go? Were parts of his fiction a way of getting back at the aunts who brought him up in early life? Unlikely. In the first place, as Wodehouse himself pointed out, in many cases it was a kindness of the various aunts in England to look after three peripatetic growing boys. Any resentment there was should surely be shown to his mother for neglecting her duties. Not that his mother would see it that way, and neither necessarily should we.

When it was felt that children were more likely to remain healthy and grow into adulthood in England than the Far East, and when England was reckoned to offer better educational facilities than Hong Kong, to have the children grow up and be educated in England would seem logical even though their parents would still be living in Hong Kong. Social attitudes change over time, and it is perhaps invidious to judge people out of their context. After all, all Eleanor Wodehouse was striving to do was look after her children's health and provide them with a good education. Those are worthy aims, however clumsy the execution might seem to modern eyes.

Wodehouse and his mother did not have a close relationship. When a son could go years between sightings of his mother that is not unexpected. But when they did get together, they found they had little in common. Apart from the hindrance that they did not have shared experiences to bring them together, they did not have similar interests or hobbies which would do so either. There were few stages on which they could interact. His mother featured little in his own life, and mothers were to feature little in his fiction. Rarely dextrous when writing about emotions, he would naturally be tempted to steer clear of this particular emotionally tricky subject as he had little first-hand experience on which to draw. He was to say later in life that the children knew and saw little of their mother and, as a consequence, viewed her 'as another aunt'.

But the absence of mothers from his fiction is not that remarkable in itself. Masses of books are written without them featuring. That's no big deal. What is exceptional, though, is the predominance of aunts in the Wodehouse canon. Here the rationale gets murkier. The pat reason is that Wodehouse himself was brought up by aunts. Clearly you cannot divorce a man from the influences of his background and surroundings, but I don't buy into the idea that Wodehouse's writing career was a revenge on those who offered him homes when he was young.

The character who is most famous for his aunts and his wariness of them is Bertie Wooster. Left to his own devices, he is happy, as he himself admits, merely to 'exist beautifully'. He needs a catalyst to rouse him from a state of happy idleness, golfing, trickling about and socialising. One force is his loyalty to his friends, which will always stir him into action, albeit sometimes warily and reluctantly, otherwise it is his aunts who force him into the activity so necessary if we readers are to get a book out of his latest experiences.

Bertie Wooster is a comic creation who appears in comic novels. The infrastructures of these novels provide the comedy. Aunts provide that much better than mothers. That Bertie hides in America because he is afraid of being in the same country as his aunt can be seen as funny; were he to do so as a result of fear of his mother, it would not be. That then becomes a bit sad. Aunts, not mothers are required for comedy. So aunts are what we get. Unless the joke requires a mother, then that is what we get. In *Monkey Business* Montrose Mulliner saves a baby which has been snatched by an escaped gorilla, and finds that:

> The mother was kneeling before him, endeavouring to kiss his hand. It was not only maternal love that prompted the action. That morning she had signed up her child at seventy-five dollars a week for the forthcoming picture Tiny Fingers, and all through these long, anxious moments it had seemed as though the contract must be a total loss.

That would not be funny if the relative were an aunt. Then it would conjure up pictures of a rather unpleasant and cynical exploitation. It works as a joke because we automatically take it as granted that a mother's love is there as well.

In many respects Bertie's aunts fulfil a mother-in-law role. As a bachelor, Bertie had no mother-in-law, so Wodehouse slips an aunt or two into this part. Mothers-in-law are uniquely situated as a comic creation: they are part of the scenery and fabric of someone's life, but while that person does not have to welcome them into it, neither can they easily, under social convention, expel them. Mothers-in-law have a wonderful opportunity to be sniffy and interfering. Also the son-in-law is under no obligation to like his mother-in-law, it is all right if he merely tolerates her.

Wodehouse's upbringing must have left its imprint on him - everyone's upbringing does, so why should he be different? If one is looking for a glimpse into any feelings of resentment, Bertie's fear of his aunts may be the wrong target.

> Of affection for his children he had little. Bailey was useful in the office, and Ruth ornamental at home. They satisfied him. He had never troubled to study their characters. It had never occurred to him to wonder if they were fond of him. They formed a necessary part of his household, and beyond that he was not interested in them. [*The Coming Of Bill*]
>
> Her father had so ordered his life in relation to his children that Ruth's affection was not so deep as it might have been. [*The Coming of Bill*]

Eleanor Wodehouse was widowed in 1929, and went to live with her son, Armine, and his wife, Nella. When Armine died in 1936 Eleanor stayed on with Nella. Through all the time that her mother-in-law lived with her, Nella could only remember PG Wodehouse coming to visit his mother once, although he would encourage his step-daughter, Leonora, to do so. The above quotations can be seen as his rationalisation of why visits to his mother virtually ceased once his father had died. When, in his teenage years, Plum had got to know his father, he took to him in a way he was never to with his mother. His father and he had interests in common, both being keen on sport, and this provided a meeting place for their minds.

Conversely, he confessed that he could never think of anything to say to his mother.

If, as has been suggested, Wodehouse was hostile to his mother, then how does this argument account for his love for Ethel Rowley, someone who had a nine-year old daughter who was being educated on the opposite side of the Atlantic to her. If Wodehouse thought his mother cruel for inflicting this on him, would he have fallen in love with a woman who was following the same practice? Wodehouse had not even met his wife's daughter - who was to become his step-daughter - when he got married.

Armine was to spend his career in India, and his son, Patrick, was left in the care of two sisters who looked after the offspring of ex-pats, and who had been recommended by PG Wodehouse's friend Guy Bolton, who was later to leave his own daughter with them. Patrick was four at the time. When he was seven his mother returned for a brief spell to fix him up as a boarder at a prep school. The holidays were spent being shuttled around his relatives, one of whom was Plum whom he remembers as 'always kind and generous towards me'. [*Wooster Sauce*, June 2001]

Wodehouse himself advanced Mary and Louisa as role models for two of his literary creations. But could there be a bit of Ethel in them too? How much Wodehouse was in fact bossed by his wife is a matter of conjecture. Not as much as he claimed to be, that is certain. But Ethel had a strong personality and would force him into doing things he would rather avoid. In Ethel, PG Wodehouse often saw an excuse for his actions, rather than her actually being the true motivation. But could not this idea have seeped into his work? After all, the aunt motif only comes through strongly in his fiction after he had got married. It also coincides with the period in which he wrote comedy. If the real life aunts were the inspiration, sole or otherwise, would he not have begun writing about his memorable fictional aunts earlier?

Baby Wodehouse went back to Hong Kong with his mother. When the eldest of his brothers was six, and ripe for an English education, the three children went to England with their mother. She rented a house in Bath and hired a nanny, a Miss Roper, as governess for the children. Eleanor returned to Hong Kong and her husband leaving her children, including two-year-old Pelham, in Miss Roper's care.

In 1886 Ernest and Eleanor travelled to England as Ernest was to be invested into the companion order of St Michael and St George for his work organising the Chinese section of the Great Exposition. During this visit Mr and Mrs Wodehouse decided to move their children to a Dame school in Croydon, run by two spinsters, Florrie and Cissy Prince. There were also a couple of other children there, whose parents lived in India.

Three years into the stint at the Princes, Peveril developed a weak chest. The Channel Islands was considered the place to go to recover from such an ailment, so it was to there that Peveril was sent, along with his brothers as company. The Wodehouses were enrolled in Elizabeth College on Guernsey. After two years at Elizabeth College, Pelham was dispatched to continue his education at Malvern House, a naval prep school in Kent. For the first time the Wodehouse children were to be split up, Peveril remaining, on medical grounds, at Elizabeth College and Armine going on to Dulwich College. Behind the decision to send Pelham to Malvern House was an aunt. Aunt Edith had persuaded Ernest of the benefits of her nephew joining the navy - in which her husband, Gussie, served. Malvern House specialised in preparing pupils for the Royal Naval College, Dartmouth. A naval career was always going to be unlikely for her nephew as he had problems with his eyesight. During the First World War he twice volunteered for military service, but was rejected for this defect.

School holidays were spent being transferred among relatives. It was an age when the bringing up of children was left to the servants, so even during his brief stays with his relatives Wodehouse hardly got to know them. Of the servant class, however, Wodehouse developed a fondness. He attributed this to affection for the maids at the Princes' house when he was still very young. It was an affection which was to remain with him. In the twenties and early thirties he would frequently stay as a guest at Hunstanton Hall, and even rented it himself for a period. The parlour maid at Hunstanton, Mrs Hide, became one of the many people with whom he kept up a correspondence.

When aunts, with Pelham in tow, went visiting the neighbours, it was often suggested that young Pelham might be happier taking tea with the servants. He probably was. This was to have another benefit later in life for he understood, better than most of his class could be expected to, how the servant mind worked and how they ordered themselves. The first Blandings Castle novel is told from the point of view of those below stairs, with the hero and heroine a valet and maid and the etiquette of behaviour in the servants' hall - more stifling than those of their masters - minutely observed. These visits must have been remembered when he came to write *Spring Fever*, in which Mike Cardinal returns to a castle he used to visit as a small boy:

> 'What is this door before which we have paused?'
> 'The drawing-room. You seem to have forgotten the geography of the house.'
> 'They didn't allow me in the drawing-room much, when I was here before. Rightly or wrongly, they considered that my proper place was in the tool shed, playing ha'penny snap with Tony and the second footman.'

When Patrick Wodehouse came to stay, Plum and Ethel Wodehouse were not sure how to entertain him, and they would send him out with the footman to walk the dogs in the morning. Wodehouse's sympathetic thoughts towards domestic staff did not extend to nannies. He remembered

Miss Roper, even though he was in her charge only up to the age of five, as strict. A short story about George and Frederick Mulliner's nanny, Nurse Wilks, is entitled *Portrait Of A Disciplinarian*. She thinks nothing of locking 'Master Frederick', by now an adult, in the cupboard for not kissing his fiancée 'Miss Jane' when apologising to her, nor of shutting Jane Oliphant in the cupboard as well, for trying to smoke. But criticisms of nannies in his books can be seen less as a reaction to his own nanny as a reaction against authority. Nannies represent authority, and such figures always had a hard time of it in Wodehouse's work.

The aristocracy are generally seen as being unfit to carry out their duties. Justices of the Peace are portrayed as being self-interested. Lord Emsworth's interest in his role upholding the law of England extends no further to seeking retribution on those who threaten and endanger his pig. Edmund Haddock pronounces a defendant he was seeking to give 30 days' imprisonment to not guilty when he discovers he is the brother of his betrothed. Sir Watkyn Bassett uses his knowledge of his niece's allowance to fine her exactly the amount which will bite. Bertie Wooster - with no evidence whatsoever - is sure that Pop Bassett sticks to the fines he hands out, and eventually gets him to pay him the £5 which he fined him for pinching a policeman's helmet on boat race night.

Getting their helmets pinched on boat race night - a custom which is a given of undergraduate life in Wodehouse's fiction, but does not correspond to the reality - is one of the main functions of the English police. The police in England are bumbling and are figures of fun to be condescended to, outwitted, bullied and humiliated. They are to be pushed into ponds, have their uniforms stolen and be beaten up. In *Do Butlers Burgle Banks?*, a policeman, Claude Potter, gets shot and the main character, Mike Bond, regrets that it is not fatal. The plot of *Frozen Assets* centres on Edmund Biffen 'Biff' Christopher's attempts to prevent himself from being arrested before his thirtieth birthday so as to inherit a fortune. He is one of the heroes in the book despite his tendency to commit physical violence on the police of whatever country he might happen to be in. He cannot return to Paris because of an attack on a policeman there. We are asked to feel sympathy for his plight, not that of the unfortunate gendarme. The book opens with a scene where a deliberately unhelpful sergeant of police in a dingy little Paris police station prevents Jerry Shoesmith from getting back his wallet when he needs it.

Stilton Cheesewright uses the majesty of the law to conduct a vendetta against Bertie Wooster, whom he suspects of trying to steal Florence Craye away from him. But American policemen are depicted as being most definitely corrupt, gaining advancement both in their profession and society by bribes. When Psmith is in New York and seeks protection to go about his lawful duty he goes not to the police but to a gang leader. Any private detective in the Wodehouse canon is liable to be more crooked than those he is sent to investigate.

Indeed, there is a strong strain of anarchism in Wodehouse's fiction. Police are not to be respected, and although criminals may be thwarted in their endeavours, they never get punished for their crimes. Lies and blackmails abound. In Wodehouse's school fiction it is the schoolboys who set the tone and structure of that society, not those in authority. Sheen is punished by being sent to Coventry by his fellow schoolboys for ignoring part of the schoolboy code. Sheen later is only able to rescue his reputation, and boost the standing of the school itself, by deliberately contravening the headmaster's orders.

Do Butlers Burgle Banks? throws up all sorts of insights into Wodehouse's morality. Not only is a policeman shot, but not killed to the regret of the main character, but a hero of the book is a villain, Horace Appleby. Yet even he has his strict code, and refuses to let Charlie Yost share the proceeds of a robbery because he carried a gun. Discovering that a girl - his ex-fiancée - is locked in the safe of the bank, he telephones the owner for the combination of the lock, although realising the peril this will place him in. Contrasting with this, the action of the story takes place after the funeral of Sir Hugo Bond of Bond's Bank who was revered as a great local benefactor, with money he himself has stolen. His nephew, Mike, takes over the bank, but does not denounce his uncle:

> 'How could I after that funeral? The whole town had gone into mourning, everyone was telling everyone that there had never been anyone like him... what a noble soul... what a big hearted benefactor. Did you expect me to stand up and say "You're all wrong chaps. The man you think so highly of was a crook and a swindler"? I couldn't do it. Besides, when you're running a bank you don't shout from the rooftops that it's short two hundred thousand pounds in its funds.'

The trustees of the bank, General Sir Frederick Featherstone and Augustus Mortlake had accepted the wages of responsibility without taking on board the responsibility. These trustees, misunderstanding a comment of Mike's, are happy to think that he is going to commit suicide to get them out of a sticky position.

Mike Bond compares Sir Hugo's actions to a former schoolmate of his who was always generous at the school shop to his friends. Only later was it discovered that he 'has been helping himself right and left to the contents of his schoolmates' pockets.'

> 'Little beast!'
> 'Not at all, Gussie. He was quite a good sort. We all liked him, even after the facts were discovered. He's a member of parliament now.'

Horace Appleby, the hero of the story, ends the book engaged to be married and determined to go straight, though this not so much due to morality but a consequence of retirement. Sir Hugo's reputation is also assured. Crooks are not unmasked in Wodehouse, even unlovely ones such as Mr Slingsby in *Bill The Conqueror*, who is allowed by the hero to make his escape to America.

Flowing from this dislike of authority is a strong opposition to those who set themselves up to judge others. This may have its roots in Wodehouse's youth, when he was brought up to tight strictures on how a young gentleman should look and behave. Miss Roper's fussiness over personal attire - her charges always had to look perfect young gentlemen - can be seen to have an outlet in Jeeves' preoccupation over clothes.

'What do ties matter, Jeeves, at a time like this? Do you realise that Mr Little's domestic happiness is hanging in the scale?'
'There is no time, sir, at which ties do not matter.' [*Very Good, Jeeves*]

Jeeves' pedantry might also carry echoes of Miss Roper:

'I hold that rank is but a penny stamp.'
'Guinea stamp, sir.'
'All right, guinea stamp. Though I don't believe there is such a thing. I shouldn't have thought they came higher than five bob. Well, as I was saying, I maintain that the rank is but the guinea stamp and a girl's a girl for all that.'
'"For a' that", sir. The poet Burns wrote in the North British dialect.'
'Well "a' that", then, if you prefer it.'
'I have no preference in the matter, sir. It is simply that the poet Burns --'
'Never mind about the poet Burns.' [*Indian Summer Of An Uncle*]

Jeeves is a good guy in the chronicles, the Efficient Baxter a bad guy. But why? What are Baxter's crimes? He tries to bring order to Lord Emsworth's life, and prevents him from evading his duties. He is conscientious. He judges others more harshly than many of those he sits down to dinner with; he suspects impostors, and that he is almost invariably right does not matter. Baxter conspires against the tide of anarchism which he fears will overwhelm Blandings.

Wodehouse's big-game hunters are always ridiculous figures who set out to kill in foreign lands based on an arrogant assumption that their way of life is best and they are the most important thing there. Capt Jack Fosdyke is a particularly unappealing example of the species and his warped view is delightfully sent up:

> 'If you had led the rough, tough slam-bang, every-man-for-himself life I have, you wouldn't be frightened of gorillas. Bless my soul, I remember once in Equatorial Africa I was strolling along with my elephant gun and my trusty native bearer, 'Mlongi, and a couple of the brutes dropped out of a tree and started throwing their weight about and behaving as if the place belonged to them. I soon put a stop to that. Bang, bang, left and right, and two more skins for my collection.' [*Monkey Business*]

Captain Fosdyke is later shown to be a coward when he encounters a gorilla in Hollywood, which is, of course, only a human in a gorilla suit.

A lack of respect for others' rights and property is also a characteristic of another big-game hunter, Jane Hubbard. In order to stop an argument, she blows a hole in her host's front door with an elephant gun which she happened to be holding as she had recently shot at one of his guests from short-range - and missed - thinking he might be a burglar. Big-game hunters are always shown to be vain, risible figures:

Eustace was lying in bed listening to Jane Hubbard as she told the story of how an alligator had once got into her tent while she was camping on the banks of the Issawassi River in Central Africa ...

'And what happened then?' asked Eustace breathlessly ...

'Oh I jabbed him in the eye with a pair of nail scissors, and he went away,' said Jane Hubbard. ...

'Nail scissors!'

'It ruined them unfortunately. They were never any use again. For the rest of the trip I had to manicure myself with a hunting spear.' [*The Girl On The Boat*]

In the short story *Feet Of Clay* Capt Fosdyke is talking with Agnes Flack, whom he wants to marry because of her money:

'Ever seen the Grand National?'

'Not yet.'

'I won it a couple of times. I remember on the second occasion Lady Astor saying to me that I ought to saw off a leg to give the other fellows a chance. Lord Beaverbrook, who overheard the remark, was much amused.'

'You seem marvellous at everything.'

'I am.'

'Do you play golf?'

'Oh, rather. Scratch.'

'We might have a game tomorrow.'

'Not tomorrow. Lunching in Washington. A bore, but I can't get out of it. Harry insists.'

'Harry?'

'Truman. We'll have a game when I get back. I might be able to give you a pointer or two. Bobby Jones said to me once that he would never have won the British and American Amateur and the Open if he hadn't studied my swing.'

This distaste for people imposing their value judgements on others can also be seen in Wodehouse's dislike of communism and socialism. Communists are attacked for being hypocrites. Bingo Little's support for communism is only as deep as his love for a communist girl. Bertie Wooster, not the greatest political philosopher it is fair to say, gently points out the absurdity of his conversion:

> 'I say you don't know how I could raise fifty quid somehow do you?'
> 'Why don't you work?'
> 'Work,' said young Bingo surprised. 'What, me? No, I shall have to think of some other way. I must put at least fifty on Ocean Breeze.' [*The Inimitable Jeeves*]

Orlo Porter, a communist, bemoans his life in conversation with Bertie Wooster in *Aunts Aren't Gentlemen*:

> 'Do you know what my insurance company pays me? A pittance. Barely enough to keep body and soul together on. And I am a man who likes nice things. I want to branch out.'
> 'A Mayfair flat?'
> 'Yes.'
> 'Champagne with every meal.'
> 'Exactly.'
> 'Rolls Royces?'
> 'Those, too.'
> 'Leaving something over, of course, to slip to the hard-up proletariat. You'd like them to have whatever you don't need.'
> 'There wouldn't be anything I don't need.'

This was written by Wodehouse when in his nineties. His views were unchanging from when he was in his twenties and was explaining the political philosophy of that most eccentric and shallow of socialists, Psmith:

> 'I've just become a Socialist. It's a great scheme. You ought to be one. You work for the equal distribution of property and start by collaring all you can and sitting on it.' [*Mike*]

The extent of Psmith's addiction to the socialist cause is shown by a career which starts with him working in a bank, goes through a stage owning a magazine and then ends - as far as the reader's knowledge extends - in gaining employment as secretary to a hereditary peer. The Old Etonian and member of several gentlemen's clubs is no socialist as has been claimed by some commentators. He is as patronising to the socialist cause as he is to many of those in power over him - at least nominally - whom he encounters on his way through life. His attitude to socialism is amused contempt.

Psmith's socialism is not credible, nor was it ever meant to be. The case of Bertie's replacement manservant for Jeeves, Brinkley or Bingley, is not clear. Bertie is convinced that he is a socialist out to start a bloody class revolution at his expense. But where is the evidence? When Brinkley does decide to try to murder him religion seems to be competing with drunken derangement as the driver of his action. Indeed, a friend of mine, himself well to the left politically, found this book hilarious simply because he did not believe Brinkley was an ardent left-winger, and found much humour in Bertie's paranoia. So far so good, except that Brinkley, who is called Bingley now, re-appears in another Wooster novel where Jeeves acknowledges that Brinkley had had left-wing leanings earlier which have disappeared now that he had become a man of property himself. This, of course, fits with the general Wodehouse analysis of the motives of many left-wingers. But of Brinkley's political leaning I am genuinely not sure.

Socialists are normally sent up by Wodehouse for their self-interest disguised as an altruistic philosophy, but in the story *Archibald And The Masses* Archibald sets out to help the working classes in a patronising, ignorant and uncomprehending manner: This is another variation on the theme of wrongly applying one's own value judgements and lifestyle where it is not necessarily appropriate.

Although critics have sought to illustrate that Wodehouse was opposed to the philosophy of Nazism through his criticism of Oswald Mosley in the guise of Roderick Spode, a more imaginative and creditable argument would concern his opposition to democratic socialism and communism. That communism and fascism are seen as opposite ends of the political spectrum can be viewed as more a convenience for political abuse than as a rational analysis of their components. Communism and fascism both require an all-important, knowing state. As such, surely it can be argued that both philosophies are left wing. The further left one travels on the political slide rule the more important the state as a judge becomes. The further right one travels the less important, and the less respected the state. Margaret Thatcher's political philosophy was about 'rolling back the frontiers of the state.' If one travels to the furthermost rightward reaches of the political scale does one not find anarchism rather than fascism? (Or maybe it is simply that the political map should be drawn as points around a circle, or a U shape which almost meets at the top, rather than as a straight line.)

Anarchism has its own strains of philosophy, one of which states that any action by an individual is permitted - even murder - so long as that individual's conscience can live with it. This philosophy underpins the structure and plots of many of Wodehouse's novels. Bertie is always hamstrung precisely because his conscience is so restricting that he is frequently crippled from taking the necessary action to rid himself of whatever particular peril is plaguing him at the time. It requires him to stay engaged to girls he can't abide, court danger by rushing to friends in need, and to honour his word. Jeeves' own moral code is much looser, and so he is able to countenance a much wider scope of action. It is often through this, rather than superior intelligence, that he is able to extract Bertie from problems which Bertie was incapable of escaping on his own.

The Chimp Twists, Soapy Molloys and Percy Pillbeams of this world operate as they do because their consciences are untroubled by their actions; Appleby, though a professional crook, will not allow a girl to remain locked in a safe because his conscience cannot allow it. Wodehouse's villains are never made to pay for transgressing society's rules so far as the actions of the book are concerned, although prison sentences may be part of a character's history. If they can live with themselves that is all Wodehouse asks. A man cannot leave a taxi cab clad in the wrong-coloured shoes not because any government or police force has forbid him to, but because he himself cannot bear to countenance the idea. The rules that govern the actions of the characters in Wodehouse's world are not those of a law-enforcing and legislating body, but of the individuals themselves.

Schooldays

> To Adair, Sedleigh was almost a religion. Both his parents were dead; his guardian, with whom he spent the holidays, was a man with neuralgia at one end of him and gout at the other; and the only really pleasant times Adair had had, as far back as he could remember, he owed to Sedleigh. The place had grown on him, absorbed him. [*Mike*]

With a few technical variations, this can be seen as a statement of Wodehouse's situation. Even when established as a high-earning author, he would return to the school to report on matches for *The Alleyian*, travelling over from France to do so. When the cricket XI went through the 1938 season unbeaten, Wodehouse paid for them to have dinner in the West End and watch a show at the Palladium. Even from across the Atlantic he would follow the scores of the Dulwich teams, despite the fact that they were of a different generation and he could know little, if anything, about the person or type of player behind the names. But the romance of the place, and of his schooldays, remained with him always. In trying to explain John Carroll's emotions on unexpectedly encountering the girl he loves, Wodehouse writes:

> Only once in his life before could he remember having felt as he felt now, and that was one raw November evening at school at the close of the

football match against Marlborough when, after battling wearily through a long half-hour to preserve the slenderest of all possible leads, he had heard the referee's whistle sound through the rising mists and had stood up, bruised and battered and covered in mud, to the realisation that the game was over and won.

This passage appears in *Money For Nothing*, published when Wodehouse was 46, and 28 years out of Dulwich. Wodehouse had been a member of the first XV in his final year and *The Alleyian* noted that at 12st 6lb he was: "A heavy forward. Has improved greatly, but still inclined to slack in the scrum. Always up to take a pass. Good with his feet. Still inclined to tackle high."

Wodehouse was a good all-round school sportsman, and was a member of the cricket first eleven for two seasons. He also boxed, being noted for his scientific manner rather than his brutality. But declining eyesight curtailed his boxing career. It cannot have helped his cricket either, and it is no surprise that a great deal of this was played as a number eleven batsman. It was as a fast bowler that Wodehouse excelled. In his first season for the eleven he took seven wickets for 50 runs against Tonbridge, including the wicket of Kenneth Hutchings for 60. Hutchings was a fine schoolboy batsman who went on to play for England seven times. In his final year in the school Wodehouse played for the Remove against the Modern VI when he took the first nine wickets - eight bowled and one LBW. One of his team mates in his final season in the college XI was NA Knox, who also played for England, and was described by Sir Jack Hobbs as 'the best bowler I ever saw.' Wodehouse was to claim that one of his proudest achievements was that he used to go on to bowl before Knox, although 'he was a child of about ten then.' Knox was, in fact, three years younger than Wodehouse.

Cricket was to be a frequent setting of Wodehouse's early writing, and a feature of his social life. He became a member of Surrey County Cricket Club, and, later, was a founder member of the Hollywood CC, taking the minutes at their inaugural meeting and contributing $100 to buy equipment. By then he was 53 and a non-playing member. He had continued to play cricket long after leaving school, though. Six times he had played at Lord's for the Authors side.

> Cricket is the great safety-valve. If you like the game, and are in a position to play it at least twice a week, life can never be entirely grey. [*Mike*]

Cricket began to have less of a role in his writing when he began to aim at the American market simply because this audience would not understand it. By then a keen golfer, Wodehouse made golf the subject of his sporting short stories, often using the same plotlines as he had employed in his cricket ones. One of the staples of these stories is that something - normally ownership or rights - depends upon the outcome of a sporting encounter. For example, *Tom, Dick And Harry* is about two cricketers who agree that whoever gets the higher score in the forthcoming match can have a free hand at wooing the object of their affections, only for them both to find that she is already engaged. This is the same storyline as the golf story *The Long Hole*.

But the biggest influence Wodehouse's love of cricket had on his work came as a result of the Warwickshire County Cricket Club secretary cutting himself while shaving during a walking holiday in Yorkshire in 1910. The local doctor, having carried out remedial action, recommended a spell watching the cricket match at Hawes. The Warwickshire secretary, RV Ryder, was impressed with one of the Hawes bowlers - who, unbeknownst to him, had had an unsuccessful trial with Yorkshire - and at the end of the innings asked him if he would like to play for Warwickshire.

Being neither born nor resident in Warwickshire necessitated the bowler undertaking a two-year qualification period, and so he only played his first championship game in 1913. That season he took 106 wickets in first-class cricket. The next season was almost as productive for him - he finished with 90 wickets - but he received an accolade which was second only to being picked for England when he was selected for the Players against the Gentlemen. That year it was the highest accolade available, as England played no test matches. He took 4 for 44 in the second innings and helped the Players to victory. Pelham ('Plum') Warner, a leading figure in cricket's establishment and frequently a selector, prophesied an England career for him.

One of those who had been impressed by his bowling was Wodehouse. He watched Warwickshire play Gloucestershire at Cheltenham in 1913 when he was down visiting his parents. He had been taken by the player's bowling action - described by *Wisden* as 'an easy action' - rather than his performance, for the bowler only took one wicket in the match. When he was hunting around for a character name he remembered this bowler, Percy Jeeves, and gave the character his surname. The first Jeeves story appeared in America in September 1915, and four months later in Britain. Six months after this, Percy Jeeves was killed at the Battle of the Somme, leaving behind according some accounts a fiancée in Annie Austin, the younger sister of the Warwickshire scorer. She lived into her eighties, but never married. 'He was very popular among his fellow cricketers' recorded *Wisden* in its obituary. Fifty-nine years later, Reginald Jeeves' creator was also to have his death recorded in *Wisden*, as 'a member of the Dulwich College XI in 1899 and 1900' and 'godfather of MG Griffith the late Captain of Sussex.'

MG Griffith was christened 'Mike', as opposed to Michael, after Wodehouse's schoolboy cricketer. His father was a friend of Wodehouse's, a friendship which arose through both attending Dulwich College, though they were not contemporaries. This is a neat reversal of the more common habit of cricketers giving their names to fictional characters, of whom Sherlock Holmes is another example. Sherlock Holmes - originally called Sherringford Holmes and then Sherrington Hope - gained his Christian name from an amalgamation of the names of two Nottinghamshire players, Mordecai Sherwin and Frank Shacklock. Sherlock Holmes' brother, Mycroft, was named after Thomas and William Mycroft of Derbyshire and Dr Roylott, who appears in *The Adventure Of The Speckled Band*, came from a corruption of the name of Arnold Rylott, a Leicestershire cricketer. Lord Ickenham is Frederick Altamont Cornwallis Twistleton. Altamont was an alias used by Sherlock Holmes.

Recollecting his schooldays with Bill Townend, Wodehouse remembered waiting at the station for *The Strand* so as to read the latest Sherlock Holmes story. Later, Wodehouse and Doyle became friends as well as fellow contributors to *The Strand*. Indeed, Doyle was his captain on the occasion of Wodehouse's greatest triumph as a batsman, when he scored sixty runs from the number four position for the Authors against the Publishers at Lord's in 1911. When Wodehouse wrote: 'isn't there enough sadness in life without going out of your way to fasten long planks to your feet and jumping off mountains' [*Young Men In Spats*] he is poking fun at his friend, who was a keen skier. Wodehouse's books are speckled with phrases which are quotations and adaptations from Sherlock Holmes. In *Right Ho, Jeeves*, Bertie sets himself up as a form of consulting practice, obviously strongly influenced by his readings of Sherlock Holmes: ('You know my methods, Jeeves. Apply them.' 'Tell me the whole story in your own words,' I said. 'Omitting no detail, however apparently slight, for one never knows how important the most trivial detail may be.') Jeeves, in the end, has the last laugh. In planning Bertie's discomfort he picks up on Bertie's fascination with Sherlock Holmes to persuade him to raise a fire alarm in the night: 'Possibly you may recollect that it was an axiom of the late Sir

Arthur Conan Doyle's fictional detective, Sherlock Holmes, that the instinct of everyone, upon an alarm of fire, is to save the object dearest to them.'

Mystery stories were some of Wodehouse's favourite reading throughout his life, and he was happy to give those authors he liked a boost in his own writings. In *The Spot Of Art*, Lucius Pim tells Bertie Wooster that 'it is impossible not to be thrilled by Edgar Wallace.' Rex Stout gets similar approval in *Much Obliged, Jeeves*.

Bearing in mind Wodehouse's love of mystery stories and his massive output, many have questioned why Wodehouse did not write this type of story himself. Erroneously, they have suggested that his facility in drawing out intricate plots for his farces would mean that he would be a good plotter of a detective novel. But farce plots are very different from detective ones. Wodehouse's plots were always very mechanical: if A happens then B will follow. This is stated as a fact and the readers know that it will happen. If the policeman is pushed into the pond then he will decide that being a copper is too dangerous and will give up the force. But detective stories rely upon doubt, of readers nosing around at the edges. A Wodehouse comic novel does not encourage this. If you do so, you will find some rather rough edges. This is not so much a critique of Wodehouse, but of the genre.

Two other factors, more specific to Wodehouse, would also militate against success as a mystery writer. The first is that he was not a great originator: he far preferred to be an adapter, whether of plots, scenarios, phrases or characters. He liked always to have some form of template to work from. Whether he would have been happy dreaming up original plots with novel resolutions is extremely doubtful. Agatha Christie, another writer whose work Wodehouse enjoyed, made her reputation not on the brilliance of her prose, but on the ingenuity of the identification of her criminals. Wodehouse's reputation rests very much on the opposite - on the brilliance of his language, not on the unexpectedness of his plots.

A second hindrance would be Wodehouse's lack of attention to detail, or indifference to it. What is the Christian name of Psmith? Wodehouse calls him both Rupert and Ronald. Is Lord Emsworth's favourite book written by Whiffle or Whipple? Does this author recommend a daily intake of 5,700 or 57,000 calories? Was Jeeves' replacement as manservant called Brinkley or Bingley? Was Bertie Wooster's prep school headmaster Aubrey Upjohn or Arnold Abney? Does Lord Emsworth like tea or not? What does Freddie Threepwood look like? Is he slim and blond or heavy and loutish looking? Is Monty Bodkin, Montague or Montrose and is he the nephew of Sir Gregory Parsloe-Parsloe or not? How many people does it take to manhandle the Empress of Blandings - one or two? How do you travel overland to Madeira when it is an island? Is the Market Blandings taxi driver Jno. or Ed. Robinson? How can *Something Fresh* be set between the hunting and shooting seasons when they overlap? How could Lord Emsworth have won a prize for tulips at the same time as Psmith's father won a prize for roses when these seasons do not overlap? How can Lord Emsworth's maternal grandmother be the Countess of Emsworth? How could Psmith, an alumnus of two public schools and a member of six London clubs, stay at Blandings confident of not being recognised as an impostor when the house was filling up with guests coming for the County Ball?

For all of these multiple-choice questions both answers are correct, depending on which book you happen to choose to find your answer from. Wodehouse explained that Psmith had his Christian name changed in *Leave It To Psmith* as Baxter was in that book and was given the name Rupert, so Psmith ceases to have the name of Rupert so as not to have two characters with the same first name. But why on earth can't two characters who are always referred to by their surname have the same Christian name?

Bertie's replacement manservant for Jeeves is called Brinkley in *Thank You, Jeeves*. In *Much Obliged, Jeeves* he is called Bingley. The reason for this is presumably that Brinkley was a name Wodehouse had already used when he christened Aunt Dahlia's house. As *Much Obliged, Jeeves* is set at Brinkley, he perhaps decided he could not have a character with the name Brinkley as well. Why is not clear. Surely the social-climbing former valet having a name similar to that of the great house of the area could be a source of humour? Instead Wodehouse just changes the name of his character. This is the action of a man indifferent to detail. In picking Bingley, Wodehouse was selecting a name he had broken in. By that stage he had written about Teddy Bingley, a golfer who appears in *Wilton's Holiday*; Gladys Bingley, Lancelot Mulliner's fiancée; Bingley Crocker, the baseball-loving father of Piccadilly Jim; the golfer Marcelle Bingley; Little Johnny Bingley the adult midget child-actor; Elsa Bingley, secretary to John Shoesmith; Mrs Bingley, Lord Tilbury's former cook, and Lancelot Bingley, the rising young artist. Lower Bingley contains people of sporting blood and Bingley-on-Sea is where Frederick Mulliner's nanny lives and the Drones Club plays golf, and Bingley versus Bingley is one of the court cases which has given Sir Raymond Bastable a low opinion of the modern young woman.

Wodehouse could suffer from a lack of imagination, or maybe just interest, on occasion. He liked to fall back on the tried and tested in phrases, plots and scenarios. Who describes who as mentally negligible? Jeeves says this of Bertie Wooster, famously so, as a plot hinges upon it. But Keggs, the butler at Belpher Castle, 'did not dislike Reggie, but intellectually he considered him to be negligible'. [*A Damsel In Distress*] Aunt Agatha eats broken bottles and conducts human sacrifices at the time of the full moon, as does Mugsy Bostock and also Abe Erlanger who features in *Bring On The Girls*, a slightly fictitious autobiographical account of Wodehouse and Bolton's theatrical career; Pop Stoker merely chews broken glass. Even Wodehouse's most famous dedication, in *The Heart Of A Goof*, 'To Leonora without whose never-failing sympathy and encouragement this book would have been finished in half the time' echoes one eight years before it in the first edition of *A Gentleman Of Leisure*, when the subject was Herbert Washbrook. Subsequently the dedication in this book was made out to Douglas Fairbanks, who starred in the play of the book.

For Wodehouse, plots were increasingly something to hang his humour on. He took great care over constructing them, but they are essentially linear in construction. Lateral thinking is not encouraged. For readers of Wodehouse novels in their original English, plots are not that essential, as we read the books primarily for the joy of the language. Therefore, some slight artificiality in the plot construction does not matter. In a detective story, where plot becomes far more important, this is more of a hindrance. I struggle to understand quite what it is that readers of Wodehouse's works in translation get out of them. Logically, for them, plot must be far more important, as ideas such as 'I could see that while not exactly disgruntled, he was far from feeling gruntled' [*The Code Of The Woosters*] will lose everything in translation. For such readers of Wodehouse, presumably it is the general air of bonhomie and the richness of some of the characterisation which add the extra ingredients.

An idea of what Wodehouse might be like in translation for those too mono-lingual to be able to read his work in a foreign language is suggested by dramatisations of his work. These do not come off very well, simply because the richness of Wodehouse's language and of his descriptions and scene-setting are lost. In dramatisations, the plots become a larger part of the overall package, and the work suffers as a result. While Wodehouse's novels are still eagerly bought and read, the plays he wrote are rarely performed and hard to get hold of. Indeed, some have never been professionally performed.

Wodehouse was asked why he did not write mystery stories, and he replied that he did not have the ability to. This is not, as some have taken it, modesty, but realism. Wodehouse was a practical writer. Mystery stories, always popular, would have been a useful earner for the young and struggling Wodehouse looking to place his short stories in magazines. If he could sell it, he would write it.

His first book is based around a mystery story. *The Pothunters* is about - but only very slightly - some stolen cups and their recovery. A detective is called in, but his role is slight and the book concerns itself, in light of this vacuum, with other matters. Not only is detection and a detective-story plot largely absent, what there is of it does not make any sense. The first bit of detective work is when the 'tec decides that, because the breaking of the window was clumsily done, it was an amateur's effort to break into the pavilion where the cups were temporarily being stored. The next bit is when he unmasks the villain, which depends more on lucky coincidence than clever detection. The detective happened to be walking past a public house when someone comes out and drops his wallet. He picks it up for him, noticing, as he does so, that there is quite of bit of money in it. He therefore takes his photograph (how is not recorded) and shows it to the groundsman who says that the chap in the photograph had been working on the school grounds 'at the time of the robbery'. (The robbery took place at night in fact, so around the time would be more accurate.) So the detective toddles over to this chap's house, and he obligingly confesses, just as he equally obligingly seems to have allowed his picture to be taken face on from close range, or otherwise how would it be good enough for the groundsman to be able to identify him?

But, more importantly, we already know that the cups have not been sold. They are lying hidden in a wood, where a schoolboy has already discovered them, but cannot tell of his find as he was breaking bounds to be in the wood in the first place. So where has the money come from? As the cups have not been sold, no-one's wallet could be bulging with ill-gotten gains from their sale.

The other time that Wodehouse ventured into mystery writing was with the short story *Death At The Excelsior*. This was never collected into book form, and appeared in *Pearson's* in December 1914. The conclusion to this uses a neat idea, if a rather unbelievable one. But unbelievability is not really a criticism in this genre, which requires possibility rather than credibility. But the main criticism is that the reader can have no chance of deducing the method of the crime himself as important information is not given until the summing up. The plot idea is a clever one, but the conclusion to the story needs a better lead-in for it to be successful. Wodehouse himself was dissatisfied with it and complained to a friend when it was republished many years later by a magazine, as he felt it sold his reputation - which by then was substantial - short.

Being good at games means a lot at public school, both to individual and group prestige. As his school, and lifelong, friend, William Townend recollected:

> Plum was an established figure in the school, a noted athlete, a fine footballer and cricketer, a boxer; he was a school prefect, in the Classical Sixth, he had a fine voice, he edited *The Alleyian*: he was in fact, one of the most important boys in the school.

The accepted view of Wodehouse's affection for Dulwich is that, starved of parental love and attention, he found an extended family in the school, which gave his life the foundation and centre which it had so far lacked. There may well be truth in this, but the sort of family life Wodehouse had is not a prerequisite for enjoying public school life.

There is much glory to be had at public school. In sports, for either house or school, it can be found through scoring the winning try, or goal, or taking vital wickets or a crucial catch. There are privileges to be awarded, from the petty to the more significant, such as being head of college, down the ranks to school prefect, head of house, and house prefect. There are scholarships to be won, prizes to be gained, competitions to come top in, colours to be awarded, promotions in the corps to be fought over. Public school life offers all sorts of cheap glory. This can make it a very romantic time for many passing through. Clearly it was for Wodehouse.

On one of his visits to England, Ernest Wodehouse, passing through west Dulwich on the train from Victoria, saw the buildings and grounds of Dulwich College. Enraptured by their beauty, he decided to send Armine there. Visiting his brother at school, PG Wodehouse fell in love with Dulwich College and asked his father that he, too, might be sent there. His father concurred, and Wodehouse was admitted to Dulwich in May 1894.

Wodehouse started his school career by lodging at the house of an assistant master, and in September became a boarder at Escott's, which was based at Ivyholme under the care of Revd Escott-Sweet. Boarding houses in this period took their name from the housemaster, not the building. During Wodehouse's school career his father retired early from the civil service on medical grounds. A keen walker, like his third son, he had contracted severe sunstroke on a walking race in Hong Kong. The Wodehouses took a house in Dulwich, so as to be near Armine and Plum, and Plum became a day boy after a year as a boarder. Boarding is generally more fun at a school, and this Wodehouse had found. Boarders are more a part of the society of a school. Day boys tend to be around for the timetabled bits such as lessons and games, but are gone for the periods of free time when friendships are made and deepened, gossip exchanged and created. Some day boys can feel semi-detached from the school. Wodehouse much preferred being a boarder to living with his parents, even though Dulwich was primarily a day school, with boarders in the definite minority. He was not to be a day boy for long, as his parents moved to Stableford in Shropshire, and so he boarded again, this time at Treadgold's, based at Elm Lawn.

Wodehouse was on the Classical side at school, the other options beings Modern, Science and Engineering. His classical education was to serve him well as a writer, indeed he described it as 'the best form of education I could have as a writer.' However, he was not blind to its limitations. His schooling was not designed to provide a grounding for a job in commerce, which Wodehouse left Dulwich to enter. Though grateful for his own education, he could be sharp about the practical benefits of a public school syllabus. In one of his early short stories, *The Goalkeeper And The Plutocrat*, a father complains to his son that he must be able to get a job somehow:

> 'Haven't I given you the education of an English gentleman?'
> 'That's the difficulty.'

Dr Arthur Gilkes, who had become headmaster of Dulwich in 1885 and remained in this post for twenty-nine years, was both a published novelist and a classicist who taught Wodehouse. It is he to whom Wodehouse refers in *The White Feather*:

> The headmaster was silent. To him 'education' meant Classics. There was a Modern side at Wrykyn, and an Engineering side, and also a Science side; but in his heart he recognised but one Education - the Classics.

JT Sheppard, a classmate of Wodehouse's and later Provost of King's College, Cambridge, reckoned that 'no-one who had the fortune to learn Latin prose and Greek verse from Gilkes could fail to acquire a mastery of languages.' Another who was taught by Gilkes was Raymond Chandler, who arrived a term after Wodehouse left. Like Wodehouse, he retained an affection for his old school throughout his life, and Philip Marlowe takes his name from one of the houses at Dulwich. One of the tenets of Gilkes' character and education was a dislike of pretention. Chandler wrote to his publisher in 1950 that:

A Classical education helps you from being fooled by pretentiousness, which is what most current fiction is too full of... the mystery writer is looked down on as sub-literary merely because he is a mystery writer, rather than for instance a writer of social-significance twaddle. To a classicist - even a very rusty one - such an attitude is merely a parvenu insecurity.'

A recurrent theme in Wodehouse's books is the mocking of pretention, and most especially of pretentious writers; those, for instance, who require a certain size or type of paper for their work to be printed on. Wodehouse was a practical, professional writer and admired those who were like him. He enjoyed mystery stories and respected those who wrote them.

After leaving Dulwich, Chandler entered the civil service. Of 800 candidates in the entrance exam he came top in the classics paper. Chandler served only six months as a civil servant, before returning to Dulwich to teach for a term. Wodehouse was not as able a classicist as Chandler, but he was a very competent one and might have achieved more had he had more motivation. When he learnt that he would not be going on to university, his attention to his work may have slackened. Bill Townend remembers Wodehouse's attitude to prep, when they would work at the same table:

We were supposed to prepare our lessons for the next day. I don't remember that Plum ever did. He worked, if he worked at all, supremely fast, writing Latin and Greek verses as rapidly as he wrote English. This is my recollection. But certainly the two hours were not filled entirely with work: we talked incessantly about books and writing. Plum's talk was exhilarating. I had never known such talk. Even at the age of 17 he could discuss lucidly writers of whom I had never heard... And from the first time I met him he had decided to write. He never swerved.

The ability to work quickly was one he took with him into adulthood and his writing career. Without it, his prodigious output would have been impossible. It cannot be said that Wodehouse's education made him a writer. He would have become one anyway. Nor can his Dulwich education be said to have turned out a writing genius, for Wodehouse served a long apprenticeship as a professional writer before anyone was to see anything in the way of consistent genius from him. Had Wodehouse died when he was in his early 30s no-one would be reading him now.

Wodehouse took a lot from Dulwich. Not least because it became a template for his stories of public-school life, with which he began his career as an author. His public schools, in ethos and geography, were modelled on Dulwich; his characters studied the classics and excelled at sports, as did the author. To establish Ruthven as the villain of *The Gold Bat*, we need be told no more than that he says 'thank goodness' for the doctor's certificate which prevents him from playing games.

Wodehouse had six books of school stories published before *Mike*. Can we see in them a nascent genius? It is a hard question to answer, if only because we think we know the answer already. Perhaps a better question to ask is, if we had read these books, and we were told the writer went onto write 'adult' and comic novels, would we hunt them out? I think, in my case, the answer would be no, but if I came across one when seeking something to read then I would try it.

I enjoyed all of these half-dozen books in themselves, but more interesting to me were the parts where I came across the stirrings of something recognisable. In Charteris and Clowes there are traces of an embryo Psmith.

'Can you tell *me*,' went on Charteris, 'if you have seen such a thing as a boy in the Spinney lately. We happen to have lost one. An ordinary boy. No special markings.' [*The Pothunters*]

> Nobody so much as smiled. Nobody ever did smile at Clowes' essays in wit, perhaps because of the solemn, almost sad, tone of voice in which he delivered them. [*The Gold Bat*]

We can also see the problems Wodehouse had with plotting, which were to worry him all his writing life. *The Pothunters* rapidly loses sight of its mystery story and becomes concerned with more routine events at the school. All his school stories were first destined for serialisation, which explains the markedly episodic nature of the work. A chapter contains a distinct event, and sometimes it is hard to see what this has to do with the greater whole. Chapter ten of *The Gold Bat*, 'Being A Chapter Of Accidents', has little to do with the storyline, and is a comic set piece which never quite catches fire, unlike the chimney in the story. Sports contests are described in detail, a habit Wodehouse also indulged in with his golfing short stories. By the time his golf stories came out Wodehouse was established as a comic writer, but too often within his golfing stories there is a detailed description of a match written without humour and where the details are irrelevant to the plot. This also applies to his school stories, though to a lesser extent, partly because we expect, and accept, them more from this genre. In *A Prefect's Uncle*, the title character fails to appear after chapter nine of an eighteen-chapter book, except when a letter from him is read out in chapter 17. *The Head Of Kay's* has a weak plot wherein problems do not resolve themselves other than by external happenings. The central characters do not drive the plot, and the final chapter is just a dull report of sporting encounters. Plots are generally thin, and it often takes a lot of words to advance them - for instance, in *The Gold Bat*, when Shoeblossom sees a night-time figure it takes a whole chapter to tell this story.

These books also establish certain principles which were to be a staple of Wodehouse's plots until his death. Honour is paramount at school. This is central to the whole plot of

The White Feather, but all his school stories depend upon it in some way. A character's own sense of what is right and wrong propels him through life, and external authority is to be outwitted and ignored. It is the boys who carry the true authority, as what they decide is what has to be obeyed. CS Forester is another writer who attended Gilkes' Dulwich, entering the college in 1915. In *Long Before Forty* he recollects:

> Most of the school rules were enforced not by Authority, but by the boys themselves and it was the boys who decided whether other rules should be observed at all. Soon after my arrival the Master issued a decree that in future boys might wear soft collars - mounting laundry costs and a shortage of starch had done their work. But in all the time I was there I never saw a soft collar worn. Public opinion had decided against soft collars and public opinion saw to it that they were not worn.

Much of the literary criticism of Wodehouse's school stories has centred on how he bucked the trend in not writing moralising tales for the improvement of young minds. Wodehouse wrote, as he was always to, to entertain. Anything else comes secondary. But he was not beyond a bit of moralising in these books, often in earnest, sometimes with a distinct spin on the 'advice' he was dolling out to the young.

> To smoke at school is to insult the divine weed. When you are obliged to smoke in odd corners, fearing every moment that you will be discovered, the whole meaning, poetry, romance of a pipe vanishes, and you become like those lost beings who smoke when they are running to catch trains. The boy who smokes at school is bound to come to a bad end. He will degenerate gradually into a person that plays dominoes in the smoking-rooms of ABC shops

with friends who wear bowler hats and frock coats.
[*The Gold Bat*]

Perhaps the difference is that when other authors passed on their tips and advice for the improvement of the young, they did so in the guise of a strict guardian; even, dare we say it, of an aunt. When Wodehouse did this, it was as an elder brother.

Strangers always look big on a football field. When you have grown accustomed to a person's appearance, he does not look nearly so large. [*The Gold Bat*]

Not that it was always to the schoolboys that his advice was directed:

There is usually one house in every school of the black sheep sort, and if you go to the root of the matter, you will generally find the fault is with the master of that house. A house-master who enters into the life of the house, coaches them at games, umpiring at cricket and refereeing at football, never finds much difficulty in keeping order. [*The Gold Bat*]

Psmith first appears in Wodehouse's twelfth book, published when he was a month short of his 28th birthday, and is Wodehouse's first great character. He enters in the second half of *Mike* and lights up the novel with his language, coolness and outwitting of all authority whether his own housemaster or Mr Downing or the established and expected traditions of the school. Psmith is in love with himself and seeks to order his life for personal amusement. When he sends himself up, as he likes to, it is not so much modesty which motivates him but the feeling that he is someone who is important enough to be sent up.

Mike was the conjunction of two serials from *The Captain*, *Jackson Junior* and *The Lost Lambs*. Subsequently split up again, they are now published as *Mike At Wrykn* and *Mike And Psmith*. Wodehouse claimed that Psmith was the only character which came to him ready made, being based on someone who was at school with a cousin of his, who wore a monocle, was immaculate in his attire and called everyone 'Comrade.' Wodehouse said this man is Rupert D'Oyly Carte. However, Rupert D'Oyly Carte's daughter suggested that the description better fitted Rupert's elder brother, Lucas.

In claiming that Psmith came fully formed as a character, Wodehouse is being disingenuous. Having never met this man, he had to fill in the considerable gaps from his imagination. What it gave Wodehouse was a template to work from, always his favourite form of construction. Many of his other characters are based on either an acquaintance or a stock character. What Psmith gave Wodehouse was the chance to construct his first really memorable individual. Wodehouse's relief at achieving this has perhaps caused this piece of faulty recollection-cum-analysis.

Perhaps as important is that *Mike* was written after he had already moved on from school stories to adult novels. Psmith dominates *Mike* partly because he is a strange schoolboy. In attitude, self-confidence and patronisation of things he finds absurd, he brings an adult perception to public-school life. He works so well as a schoolboy character because he is only partly a schoolboy. He is a hybrid character and this flows through into the book, which is less of a traditional school story than his previous five full-length tales - *Tales Of St Austin's* being a collection of short stories and essays. Wodehouse retained affection for *Mike* throughout his life, and it is a gem - well the latter half is, once Psmith has made his appearance.

There is something glorious in the way Psmith courts disaster with such aplomb, and always triumphs. Even when he is being shot at or kidnapped by New York gangsters there appears to be little danger. His defiance of authority with such ease and success provides a bit of wish-fulfilment for all of us. Stuck in a job he dislikes - and who has not been there at some time - he merely treats it as a joke, not against him, as the rest of us would, but one provided for his benefit.

Psmith is the most anti-authoritarian of Wodehouse's characters, if one excludes the genuine criminals. But he has no political agenda; he is out for Psmith, but not in a cruel way. He has discovered a game which he enjoys and is good at. In *Mike* he is anti the public school system. In *Psmith In The City* it is the bank manager who takes Psmith on in his bank so as to humiliate him; Psmith eagerly takes up the battle and humiliates the bank manager instead. In *Psmith, Journalist* he takes on the complacency of *Cosy Moments* and slum landlords. But there is no fire in his belly. This is a campaign he wages, albeit with great bravery and determination, as a diverting holiday job. He has no real interest in cleaning up the corruption of New York politics or of tenement housing. It is more something to while away the time, as he had found traipsing after his friend watching him play cricket not diverting enough. After three books - or two and half if you like - Wodehouse would probably have happily abandoned his creation. Psmith needed enemies to fight, and they were not readily apparent. He had become a rebel without a cause.

Instead Psmith reappears fifteen years, and seventeen books after his third outing. Wodehouse's daughter, Leonora, had urged her father to write another Psmith story and *Leave It To Psmith* is the result. By now Mike is just the provider of a plot line and gets only the tiniest of walk-on parts. Mike is a dull personality, whose dullness serves to allow Psmith to project his light even brighter. But by now Wodehouse had no need of him. The Psmith in this book is a different creature from what he was during his schoolboy-to-undergraduate stage. He no longer has targets to bounce off. There is no enemy he can fit into his sights, and no longer does he have the weaponry. Previously he was buttressed by his father's money. This gave him the ability to outwit his enemies through simple financial muscle; he can transform *Cosy Moments* and use its editorial pages to wage war against slum landlords only because his father has so much money he is prepared to buy the magazine title for him. What happens to Psmith's ownership of this magazine after he leaves America is not clear. We must presume, such is Psmith's financial and employment situation, that he no longer has any connection with it. Psmith can outfox the bank manager because his father has bought him a membership of the same London club that the bank manager belongs to, and Psmith can beard the bank manager in his lair. Psmith can ensure that Mike achieves his wish to go to university through getting his father to finance his friend through university on the promise of a land agent's job upon graduation.

But by *Leave It To Psmith*, the father has gone and his money with him. Psmith has nothing to oppose, so instead he sets out on a more positive purpose - wooing the girl he loves. When he achieves this he is, from the novelist's point of view, left with nothing. He is accordingly retired permanently.

Married men have little of the narrative meat in Wodehouse's books. Normally the only job for a married man is to be bullied by his wife, who is often the one who holds the purse strings. Married men do not have the room for manoeuvre that Wodehouse requires for his lead characters. Ukridge was de-wifed for this purpose, and is a much better character as a result. A married Psmith - what would he do? The only way Wodehouse could get him back into the action was if his wife were elsewhere, he found himself with time on his hands with which to amuse himself, and could resurrect some of his youthful impetuosity and gentle mischief making. There is a strong case, therefore, to suggest that Psmith did come back, but as Lord Ickenham.

Lord Ickenham is an extension of the Psmith in the final novel, not of the earlier ones. Lord Ickenham has no enemies, only a desire to stave off boredom in whatever reckless manner takes his fancy. Wodehouse's best short story - an opinion backed by a survey of the members of all the Wodehouse societies worldwide - is *Uncle Fred Flits By*, where

Lord Ickenham creates amiable havoc and confusion simply for the sheer hell of it, as a pleasurable way to spend a rainy afternoon. Here he was being self-indulgent, normally he is well-motivated in his schemes - what he calls his efforts to 'spread sweetness and light.' Psmith can also be self-indulgent, but also acts altruistically. But both of them only set out to be altruistic in such a manner that will allow them to have plenty of fun along the way. Lord Ickenham enters the canon impersonating other people, just as Psmith had spent his final book at Blandings Castle in the guise of Ralston McTodd, a Canadian poet. When Uncle Fred is given a novel to star in, he heads for Blandings in the guise of Sir Roderick Glossop, noted loony doctor. He is retracing Psmith's footsteps. Like Psmith, he is thin of build and sends himself up. Psmith claims to be shy and poor with words and Lord Ickenham gives this inaccurate self-analysis to his long-suffering nephew Pongo:

> The quiet rural life does have a wonderful effect on people. Take me. There are times, I admit, when being cooped up at Ickenham makes me feel like a caged skylark, though not of course looking like one, but there is no question that it has been the making of me. I attribute to it the fact that I have become the steady, sensible, perhaps rather stodgy man I am today. I beg your pardon? [*Cocktail Time*]

Psmith, recounting the brief story of his life to Miss Clarkson, says:

> When I was but a babe, my eldest sister was bribed with sixpence an hour by my nurse to keep an eye on me and see that I did not raise Cain. At the end of the first day she struck for a shilling, and got it. [*Leave It To Psmith*]

Lord Ickenham's infancy was not dissimilar:

'My personal attendants generally left me at the end of the first month, glad to see the last of me. They let me go and presently called the rest of the watch together and thanked God they were rid of a knave.' [*Cocktail Time*]

For Psmith, conversation acts like a mental stimulus. He gets ideas while talking and we cannot be certain that he knows where he is going with any train of thought, only that he is enjoying the journey. Psmith is frequently described as a 'buzzer'. Lord Ickenham can buzz with the best of them, and when he is in danger of being exposed by a police constable who knows the real Major Brabazon-Plank, and so is aware that Lord Ickenham is not he, his lordship rallies superbly with a feast of world play Psmith would be envious of:

'Just a slip of the tongue, such as often occurs. He meant Brabazon-Plank, *major*. As opposed to my brother, who, being younger than me, is, of course, Brabazon-Plank, *minor*. I can understand you being confused,' said Lord Ickenham with a commiserating glance at the officer, into whose face had crept the boiled look of one who finds the conversation becoming obtuse. Three kippers, four eggs and half a loaf of bread, while nourishing the body, take the keen edge off the mental powers. 'And what makes it all the more complex is that as I myself am a mining engineer by profession, anyone who wants to get straight on the Brabazon-Plank situation has got to keep steadily before them the fact that the minor is a major and the major is a miner. I have known strong men to break down on realising this. So you know my minor, the major do you? Most interesting. It's a small world, I often say. Well, when I say "often", perhaps once a fortnight. Why are you looking like a stuffed pig Bill Oakshott?' [*Uncle Dynamite*]

As with Psmith, Wodehouse was not sure what to do with Uncle Fred. He only gives him four novels, and he gets two of these only by being slotted into the role Gally more customarily plays at Blandings. In his second novel, *Uncle Dynamite*, the characterisation goes a bit askew. Why is Uncle Fred a stranger to a near neighbour of long standing? He excuses himself by saying that he tries to avoid society in the country, but how does this fit with his desire for adventure and his longing for an audience for his word-play? Also, how has he gathered such an impressive local reputation for eccentricity under such a handicap? With Wodehouse, plot was paramount and characters do what the plot requires of them. But the Uncle Fred of this novel does not fit with what we expect of him.

Psmith appeared in only three-and-a-bit works, as he gets only half of *Mike* and Uncle Fred manages only four and a very-little-bit as he only gets one short story in *Young Men In Spats*. Lord Ickenham is in the tradition of Psmith, and worthy of the former's creator. He is Psmith without the edge, but then so, too, was Psmith by the time of *Leave It To Psmith*.

Banker

It was intended that Wodehouse would take the scholarship entrance exam for Oriel College, Oxford. Armine had already gone up to Oxford University, having won a classics scholarship to Corpus Christi, and went on to take a first-class degree and win the Newdigate Prize for Poetry and the Chancellor's Essay Prize. But a reversal in the family fortunes meant that his father felt that he could not afford to send another son to university.

One wonders how closely Ernest Wodehouse did his sums. Indeed, one must question whether he made the decision through accurate economic analysis or just from innate caution. Ernest Wodehouse was not destitute, but a falling exchange rate had reduced his pension to £900 a year. Perhaps he feared that it might fall further due to exchange-rate fluctuations, and that he was unable to undertake long-term financial planning. However, he did feel comfortable enough to give Plum an annual allowance of £80. As Dulwich College would have given Wodehouse an award of up to £30 a year, as it did for all students going up to Oxford, this meant there would have between £80 and £110 a year available to him for his expenses whilst at university.

Against this had to be set his costs. To a limited extent, undergraduates could determine these themselves. There was no standard set termly fee and each undergraduate would run his own account with the college. Therefore, those of more straitened means could economise by leading a less lavish lifestyle; for example, by renting one of the cheaper rooms in college.

Presumably Ernest Wodehouse would have based any calculation on what it was costing Armine to be up at Oxford. In his first term at Oxford Armine ran up a bill of £45.1s 1d. Of this, the most substantial contributions were £11. 2s 7d to the kitchen for his meals, £9 for his tuition, and £6. 18s 6d in subscriptions to sporting clubs. Among the other items are £5s 6d 8d for his room rent, £1. 5s 2d for coal, faggots and gas, 1s 10d to the library, 13s 10d for a smoking concert, and, most strikingly, 16s 8d for income tax. In his first year his college bills came to just over £170; or, after his scholarship money had been deducted, £90.

Even after allowing for some extra expenses which would not appear on the college bill, these figures suggest that PG Wodehouse could have existed on an income of £80 to £110 if this figure was boosted by the award of a scholarship, which at Oriel would also have been worth £80. Wodehouse's income was also likely to be increased by earning money through journalism. As he was already earning money from writing about Dulwich while he was still there, he would undoubtedly have found Oxford fertile ground for subject matter.

The decision to withdraw him from the entrance exam to Oxford had already been taken by the time Armine had finished his second year at Corpus Christi. His aggregate bills for the year were about £155, or £75 after his Corpus Christi scholarship money had been taken into account.

That he did not go to university remained a regret of Wodehouse's. It is unlikely, however, to have affected the course of his life. He always wanted to write, and so write he would. His failure to get into university did not propel him into becoming a writer, nor would the acquisition of a university degree have prevented it. Whether Wodehouse would have become an even better writer had he spent three more years in education is hard to evaluate. It would not have hindered his writing, but whether any substantial benefit would have accrued from this time is doubtful. Wodehouse was well-read as a schoolboy, and continued to read widely throughout his life.

Wodehouse argued that he might be allowed to strike out as a freelance writer, but his parents would not countenance the idea. Instead, Ernest Wodehouse found for his son a job at the Hong Kong and Shanghai bank. As jobs go, it was a good one. The London branch of the Hong Kong and Shanghai bank was where young bankers were trained in preparation for going out East where they would be expected to become part of the management of one of the branches there. Another advantage, certainly for someone in Wodehouse's position, was that the work was not arduous. As the London branch was as much a training camp as anything else, there were more staff there than were necessary for it to function efficiently and there were slack periods, which Wodehouse would use to jot down, and work up, ideas for articles. For Wodehouse was determined to be a writer, and banking was something he wanted to get out of as soon as possible. Particularly, he needed to get out of it before it was his time to be sent out East, for he did not see how he could develop his writing career while based there.

As a result, every moment of free time was filled with writing in an attempt to build up enough of a freelance career to chuck the bank in. Wodehouse's first paid published work had appeared while he was still at Dulwich, when he had won a competition run by *The Public School Magazine* with an essay on 'Some Aspects Of Game Captaincy' which had netted him 10s 6d. At the end of his working day at the bank he would return to his lodgings, eat the evening meal which was provided with the rent, and settle down to writing articles, poems and short stories. In his two years at the bank he had eighty pieces published across a wide range of publications and had written many more which did not get into print.

Various myths have surrounded Wodehouse from this period, mainly propagated by the man himself. One was that he was a starving artist in his garret, able only to afford a roll for lunch. In fact his income was very respectable. The bank paid him £80 a year, and his father matched this sum with an allowance. On top of this, Wodehouse had his profits from his freelance writing. His bank salary and allowance combined already meant that he earned more than an assistant master at Dulwich College, and twice as much as some of the other clerks.

The second myth is that Wodehouse hated his time at the bank. *Psmith In The City* is Wodehouse's most overtly autobiographical work of fiction. Mike finds himself in the same circumstances as Wodehouse in being unexpectedly thrust into a bank when he had been anticipating going up to university. Mike has to find lodgings in London and rents

> one of those characterless rooms which are only found in furnished apartments. To Mike, used to the comforts of his bedroom at home and the cheerful simplicity of a school dormitory, it seemed the most dismal spot he had ever struck.

He heads to Dulwich to find his lodgings, encouraged by the presence of a public school there, hoping it might lead to games of cricket in the summer. Having conducted business with his pantomime dame of a landlady and paid a week's rent in advance,

> Mike wandered out of the house. A few steps took him to the railings that bounded the College grounds. It was late August, and the evenings had begun to close in. The cricket-field looked very cool and spacious in the dim light, with the school buildings looming vague and shadowy through the slight mist. The little gate by the railway bridge was not locked. He went in, and walked slowly across the turf towards the big clump of trees which marked the division between the cricket and football fields. It was

all very pleasant and soothing after the pantomime dame and her stuffy bed-sitting room. He sat down on a bench beside the second eleven telegraph-board, and looked across the ground at the pavilion. For the first time that day he began to feel really homesick. Up till now the excitement of a strange venture had borne him up; but the cricket field and the pavilion reminded him so sharply of Wrykyn. They brought home to him with a cutting distinctness the absolute finality of his break with the old order of things. Summers would come and go, matches would be played on this ground with all the glory of big scores and keen finishes; but he was done. 'He was a jolly good bat at school. Top of the school averages two years. But didn't do anything after he left. Went into the city or something.' That was what they would say of him, if they didn't forget him.

The clock on the tower over the senior block chimed quarter after quarter, but Mike sat on, thinking. It was quite late when he got up, and began to walk back to Acacia Road. He felt cold and stiff and very miserable.

This was written well after Wodehouse had left the bank. Its melancholy tone makes it an unusual passage in Wodehouse's writing. As such, it has been taken to be a part of pure autobiography. Wodehouse took digs in Chelsea, but maybe this is an adult reflecting on a visit he made to his former school just after leaving? The summer holiday was spent in Shropshire, at his parents, and he joined the bank in October. Maybe Wodehouse is remembering his emotions when he left Dulwich. But I would not guess to this either. The passage after all serves its purpose in setting the scene for the arrival of Psmith, who is set to transform Mike's state of mind, and his lodgings, by sweeping him up to stay with him in his far more palatial flat, financed by his father's money. Wodehouse admitted that, after initial problems with relocation to a different world, he found the bank a rather pleasant place. So, too, does Mike.

> Mike, as day succeeded day, began to grow accustomed to the life of the bank, and to find that it had its pleasant side after all. Whenever a number of people are working at the same thing, even though that thing is not perhaps what they would have chosen as an object in life, if left to themselves, there is bound to exist an atmosphere of good-fellowship; something akin to, though a hundred times weaker than, the public school spirit. Such a community lacks the main motive of the public school spirit which is pride in the school and its achievements. Nobody can be proud of the achievements of a bank.

Wodehouse discovered that his fellow clerks were also public school boys whose fathers could not finance a university education, and the bank ran a rugby and cricket team, both of which Wodehouse played for. After he had left the bank, he gathered together a team of journalists to play the bank side. For sentimental reasons he retained an account with the Hong Kong and Shanghai bank after he left, into which he paid any small cheques he earned.

The third myth is that Wodehouse did not understand what went on at the bank, and that money was to remain a mystery to him all his life. Barry Phelps in *PG Wodehouse: Man And Myth* has devoted considerable research to demolishing this theory. Wodehouse was to retain a keen interest in financial affairs all his life. This is understandable given that money, for him, was a measure of success. For a freelancer, money is everything. There are no status symbols to be acquired such as a key to the executive loo or a fancy job title. When he became established as a writer, his work was always first published in magazines. Thus, an alternative measure of success, sales figures, was not available until the work came out in book form. At the magazine stage, success was denoted by how much the magazine was paying him.

Translated into a modern standard of living, Wodehouse became a multi-millionaire through his writing, yet he could be mean over small sums, while on other occasions showing great generosity. Once he was powerful enough to get away with it, he demanded that his agent take only a 5% cut rather than the more usual 10%. But, conversely, Wodehouse was not materialistic. He enjoyed being extravagant toward his wife and daughter, but required little in the way of material possessions for himself. When he was taken ill on a walk and tottered into a doctor's surgery he was initially mistaken for a tramp, such was the shabbiness of his attire - no Psmith he. His motivation for writing was the joy of writing itself, which consumed him. He puzzled over why Michael Arlen abandoned writing once he had made enough money from it, and he himself was still writing on his death bed. He had no desire to project himself as a public celebrity. He was happy for his work alone to speak for him, though he would undergo interviews, which he did not enjoy, for the sound business reason of boosting sales.

Wodehouse was intelligent and self-effacing. The first attribute meant that he was perfectly able to summon the ability to cope with his banking tasks, although summoning the interest might be a bit harder - one of his colleagues remembered Wodehouse as cheerfully slapdash in his record-keeping in the postage department, where all new clerks were put to work. The second attribute meant that Wodehouse was not going to crow about it. Indeed, ever eager to exploit a situation for its humorous potential, his failure as a banker became one of his set pieces. He liked to make out that he was sacked from the bank for writing a humorous piece in the front of the new ledger, describing the grand ceremony of its opening. He was not. He left voluntarily, shortly after this incident, because he was then able to fulfil his desire to be a full-time writer.

This came about through a Dulwich connection. Learning that a former assistant master at Dulwich, William Beach-Thomas, was assistant editor of the By The Way column on *The Globe* newspaper, he applied to him for work. Beach-Thomas, remembering Wodehouse's work for *The Alleyian*, agreed to let Wodehouse stand in for him on the column when he took a day off. This first happened on 16 August 1901, when Wodehouse earned a guinea for his labours. Other odd days followed before he was offered a full week's work in April 1902. Wodehouse, telling the bank that he had neuralgia - the same reason Henry Blake-Somerset uses to excuse his absence from work in *Frozen Assets* - spent the week at *The Globe*. The duties were intense but not long. The working day on the By The Way column started at 10am and finished at midday. In this time Wodehouse had to write a set of topical verses and make humorous or facetious comments on the news of the day.

By September 1902 Wodehouse was ready to leave the bank. *The Public School Magazine*, which had published Wodehouse's first professional work, was founded by A & C Black in 1898. Its success led to George Newnes starting up *The Captain*. Later Wodehouse was to say that reading a story in this magazine set him on to the idea that he, too, could write public school stories. In January 1902 *The Public School Magazine* started serialising *The Pothunters*. In March the magazine folded, unable to cope with competition from *The Captain*, with Wodehouse's serial unfinished. A & C Black agreed to publish the full serial - which was given a hurried ending in the final issue - in book form instead. The company were to publish all of his public-school stories after they had been serialised in *The Captain*. Publication day was 18 September and Wodehouse was to receive a standard 10% royalty.

'Are you going to write another?'

'Dozens now that my time is my own.'

'Wasn't it always?'

'No, I had a job in the City and could only write at night. Writing at night after a hard day at the office is difficult.' [*Company for Henry*]

By now Wodehouse was making more from his writing than he was from his day job, and had saved £50 from his earnings. So when Beach-Thomas asked Wodehouse if he could stand in for him for a five-week spell while he took his annual holiday, Wodehouse gratefully abandoned his banking career and became a full-time writer. He was to remain one for 72 years.

That September the bank clerk on £6.13s a month, was transformed into a full-time journalist who had made £16.4s in his first month, a published author in book form and a contributor to *Punch*, which published its first article by him the day before his first book came out.

Wodehouse in his early years was as much a journalist as an author. It short, he was a hack, turning out anything and everything he could to make a pound. He worked quickly and with dedication. Happy with his own company, as he was to be all his life, he did not have an active social life to distract him, though he was a keen and regular games player. As industrious an author as a journalist, he had ten more books published in the six-and-half years after *The Pothunters* came out. And a varied collection they were too, including five more public-school tales, a children's story, a collection of pieces from *The Globe*, two adult novels and a 22,000-word book written in five days aimed at the railway bookshop market as light reading for a journey.

The children's story was *William Tell Told Again*, a reworking of a Swiss legend, for which Wodehouse was commissioned to write some text to accompany pictures by Philip Dadd and verses by John W. Houghton. It was the only children's story he was to write, but the first of several books where the plot was already given to him and he merely had to put it into words.

The Swoop, Or How Clarence Saved England, is even more of an oddity in Wodehouse's extensive canon. This was his reaction to the invasion-scare stories which were proving a profitable literary sub-genre at the time. These books sought to shake the British out of what their authors perceived as complacency towards German aggression and the threat of invasion and the nation's lack of military preparedness.

Wodehouse saw another motive in this flourishing publishing activity, as he explains in his introduction to the book, which was published by Alston Rivers:

> It is necessary that England should be roused to a sense of her peril, and only by setting down without flinching the probable results of an invasion can this be done. The story, I may mention, has been written and published purely from a feeling of patriotism and duty. Mr Alston Rivers' sensitive soul will be jarred to its foundations if it is a financial success. So will mine. After all, at the worst, it is a small sacrifice to make for our country.

In *The Swoop*, nine foreign forces, including the Swiss navy, independently invade Britain at the same time, and 14-year old Clarence Chugwater, using his boy-scout training, comes to the rescue of his homeland. When the Germans arrive at his front door, his father tries to let the house to them, his elder brother endeavours to sell them life insurance, his younger brother wants them to buy his motor bike and his sisters attempt to interest them in buying tickets for a concert.

Britain is relaxed about these foreign invaders, the stop press of Clarence's newspaper only carrying the news of the German army invading Essex after it has given the cricket scores. But eventually the British are forced to take these foreigners in their midst seriously as the troops of Prince Otto had done grievous damage. Cricket pitches had been trampled down, and in many cases even golf-greens dented by the iron heel of the invader, who rarely, if ever, replaced the divot. Fishing was at a standstill. Croquet had been given up in despair. Near Epping the Russians shot a fox.

The commanders of the invading armies are signed on as music hall acts, and argue among themselves as to the size of their fees. When Clarence eventually rids the country of the invaders, he is rewarded by being given a music hall turn himself.

In 1903 Wodehouse was visited by Herbert Westbrook, a prep-school master who wanted to make a career as a writer, with a letter of introduction from one of Wodehouse's former colleagues in the bank. A friendship sprang up between the two men, and Wodehouse was invited to visit him at his school. This establishment was eccentrically run by Baldwin King-Hall, a cricket fanatic who used to hold a morning meeting from his bed at ten o'clock while he ate his breakfast. Baldwin-King and Wodehouse also took to each other and Wodehouse left his Chelsea lodgings to move to Emsworth House where he took rooms above the stables. Wodehouse took no part in the teaching, but helped to put on plays and played in cricket matches on the school grounds.

Westbrook was a classicist with great charm and ambitious plans for the future. He had a communal attitude to property, but only in the sense of what's yours is mine, for he would borrow money without intending to pay it back, and on one occasion borrowed Wodehouse's dress clothes, leaving their rightful owner, who had needed them that night, to go out attired in the suit of an uncle of an entirely different build. This became raw material for the story *First Aid for Dora*.

That this is a Ukridge story is no coincidence, for Ukridge was based upon Westbrook. Or certainly the Ukridge of the short stories: the Ukridge who first appeared, in the first adult novel Wodehouse wrote, in *Love Among The Chickens*, is a slightly different beast. The Ukridge here is an amalgam of two people, the second of whom is Carrington Craxton. He and a friend had set themselves up as chicken farmers in Devon without either of them knowing anything about chickens. Townend, a friend of Craxton's, relayed tales of some of their adventures to Wodehouse who used them as a basis for his novel. But Ukridge is not the central character in this story, it is the narrator, Jeremy Garnet.

Wodehouse was keen to establish a character for whom he could write a series of stories, and sixteen years later in Ukridge he saw someone who could be developed into such a character so Ukridge became a bachelor, more seedy and more fully drawn. Part of the style of *Love Among The Chickens* was retained in that the tales are told by a journalist friend, the bachelor James Corcoran, who inherited this role from Garnet. In other respects the style of the only Ukridge novel, which was all over the place, was abandoned. The novel starts with the story being narrated about Jeremy Garnet, then becomes narrated by him, and finishes with his wedding, which is written up in play form. When, fourteen years later, Wodehouse came to revise the work for a new edition, he made Garnet narrate the whole story, which is now minus the wedding scene. As a comic work, the novel lacks sufficient humour. It never really takes off. The situations are not developed enough. Maybe the author took the plots too closely from real life. However, it was the book which launched him in America. He had turned down an offer from a friend living in the States to help him get his school stories placed with an American publisher. He wanted to hit America as an adult writer. His school stories had served a purpose in getting him up and running in Britain and out of the bank, but they are not where he saw his long-term future.

Ukridge is the most immoral of Wodehouse's leading characters. Wodehouse loved his creation and wrote about him at intervals throughout his life. The final Ukridge short story occurs in *A Few Quick Ones*, published in 1959. The Ukridge stories divide fans of PG Wodehouse. Some simply do not care for them, mainly because they do not care for Ukridge. Rogues can be popular characters, but they normally have to be loveable rogues. Ukridge is immoral, but lacks the charm or softer side to make us like him. One of the most popular characters in the history of British television sit-com is Del Boy in *Only Fools And Horses*. He is a rogue and a crook, but has a kinder side and can be generous with his money, time and emotions. He is a sympathetic character. He is also unsuccessful, which makes us well disposed to him rather than jealous. Ukridge is also unsuccessful on the whole, although he has his minor triumphs. The problem with these minor triumphs is that sometimes his victim is not deserving. When in *Ukridge's Dog College* he does down his landlord by getting out of paying his rent and getting the landlord to settle his tradesmen's accounts do we cheer him on? What have we got against his landlord? Psmith takes as his targets the more legitimate figures of established authority. We do not mind if they are taken down a peg or two; they are high enough already. But Ukridge does down those less able to take the punishment. Ukridge sponges off his fellow strugglers.

It is hard to sympathise with Ukridge. This detracts from the stories, which are well written and crafted, and often have more plot than Wodehouse would usually use for a short story. But Wodehouse's fondness for his character is considerably above that which the average reader has. Richard Usborne in *A Wodehouse Companion* states that Ukridge contains 'some of the best stories that Wodehouse ever wrote.' The stories are probably better than our enjoyment of them. In *Wodehouse At Work* he writes 'one loves that man.' The problem is that many readers do not.

Ukridge is a liar, thief, blackmailer and con man. He has little in the way of conscience or scruples. He has few, if any, compensatory characteristics to make us like him. Corky's landlord, Bowles, approves of him and that he is good with dogs is about all you can say in his defence. It is not nearly enough. Putting the case for Ukridge might involve pointing out that, although he sets out to double-cross people, he often ends as the one who is double crossed instead. However, this does not make us feel sympathy for him; 'getting his just deserts', is a more likely reaction. It is easy to admire some of the Ukridge stories, harder to enjoy them.

Wodehouse's final school story was set at Emsworth, and called *The Eighteen Carat Kid*. With a love interest added, it came out in book form as *The Little Nugget*. Some commentators have classified this as his final school story, but, although set at a school, it is written from an adult perspective and is an adventure rather than a school story. Again, the plotting has some holes in it. There are the odd daft premises, such as how White the butler exposes the schoolmaster Burns as a kidnapper, when Burns could as easily expose White as Smooth Sam Fisher, the head of a criminal gang, and also at the school as a kidnapper. The set-up and the action are artificial, and why is Miss Sheridan, whose job is to look after the Little Nugget, still at the school when he had been kidnapped days before? It is this book which sets one of the standard patterns of Wodehouse: there is the country house and its grounds where the majority of the action takes place, and there is London. No other places exist. So when the Little Nugget has gone, it is taken as read that it is to London he has ventured.

Between 1903 and 1914 Wodehouse spent a lot of time at Emsworth. He moved from above the stables into a house called Threepwood in 1904. In the autumn of 1904 Beach-Thomas resigned from his position as assistant editor of the By The Way column and Wodehouse became his replacement. The holiday relief cover job Wodehouse gave to Westbrook. A year later the editor resigned and Wodehouse took on his job. Westbrook became his assistant and William Townend became the holiday cover.

With Westbrook, Wodehouse collaborated on a novel which was published as *Not George Washington*. The plot concerns a young man trying to establish himself in London as a successful writer. The man is James Orlebar Cloyster who lives at 23 Walpole Street in Chelsea, where Wodehouse had digs, and works for a London evening paper *The Orb* where he writes the 'On Your Way' column. As with Wodehouse, the first humorous article he had published was called 'Men Who Missed Their Own Weddings'. Wodehouse was employed by the actor-manager Seymour Hicks and worked on *The Beauty of Bath* at the Hicks Theatre; Cloyster is employed by the actor-manager Stanley Briggs to work on *The Belle of Wells* at the Briggs Theatre.

Cloyster's fiancée lives in Guernsey, where Wodehouse was schooled. Cloyster will marry her when he becomes a success and to hide his achievements he writes articles under a friend's name. This is a tactic Wodehouse himself used, presumably recognising that magazines did not want too many Wodehouse bylines in any one issue. Later, when he worked on *Vanity Fair*, he would write great chunks of the magazine himself, but many of these articles would appear under *nom de plumes*, some of them rather transparent, such as Pelham Grenville and J. Plum. *Not George Washington* was divided into thirds with a different narrator for each; the first narrator was the fiancée. Although he experimented with female narrators in some of his earliest work, he was happier speaking with a male voice about male attitudes and would always employ a male character when he used a narrator in his later work.

Another collaboration was with Charles Bovill on *A Man of Means*, about the adventures of a man who comes in to a great deal of money, which ran in *The Strand* from April to September 1914. The pair had devised the plots together, and Wodehouse had written them up. The series stopped when war left Wodehouse stranded in America and his collaborator in England.

America

Wodehouse first visited America in 1904, when he took his five weeks' annual holiday from *The Globe* and went to stay in New York with a friend from his banking days. He also visited the training camp of the middleweight boxer 'Kid' McCoy, who was preparing for a title fight with 'Philadelphia' Jack O'Brien. In his reminiscences, Wodehouse claimed that boxing was the lure which took him across to America. So, too, would have been the knowledge that America had a flourishing English-language publishing industry, attractive to any freelancer.

> Jerry's got vision. He realised that the only way for a writer to make a packet nowadays is to muscle in on the American market, so he took time off and dashed over there to study it. [*Pigs Have Wings*]

He sold a series of stories about the boxer Kid Brady, which appeared from September 1905 onwards, and brought him $50 an episode, £10 under the then dollar-sterling exchange rate. His American jaunt also helped him become more marketable to English publishers. Now he could sell his expertise on, and understanding of, matters in America. In August *Punch* published his article 'Society Whispers From The States'. As Lady Malvern explains in *Jeeves And The Unbidden Guest*:

> No doubt you have read *India and the Indians*? My publishers are anxious for me to write a companion

volume on the United States. I shall not be able to spend more than a month in the country, as I have to get back for the season, but a month should be ample. I was less than a month in India, and my dear friend Sir Roger Cremore wrote his *America from Within* after a stay of only two weeks.

Lady Malvern, indeed, might be been seen as a rather slow and over-fussy researcher when compared with her peer group:

He had been introduced to an elderly and adhesive baronet, who had recently spent ten days in New York, and escape had not been without a struggle. The baronet, on his return to England, had published a book entitled 'Modern America and its People' and it was with regard to the opinions expressed in this volume that he wanted Jimmy's views. [*A Gentleman of Leisure*]

Wodehouse's second visit to America was in 1909. He had had *Love Among The Chickens* published in May of that year, but the money from the man appointed to be his agent was not forthcoming and this provided strong motivation for returning. Shortly after arriving, Wodehouse sold a short story for $200 and another for $300. These were fees well beyond his English experience, so he wired his resignation to *The Globe* and settled down in America to make his fortune. Or so he hoped.

In New York one may find every class of paper which the imagination can conceive. [*Psmith, Journalist*]

Despite his industry, Wodehouse was unable to establish any writing contacts as strong as he had with some of his

English publishers, and so returned to England in 1910 and took up with *The Globe* again.

That year *A Gentleman Of Leisure* was published. It was a significant stage in Wodehouse's development as a writer as it was his thirteenth book to be published, but only his second in America. American readers actually got the book five months earlier than the British. For the first time Wodehouse combines English and American characters and English and American settings. He was aiming fair square at marketing his book on both sides of the Atlantic.

The story sought to capitalise on the fashion for gentleman burglars of the Raffles type. American Jimmy Pitt, the gentleman of leisure of the title, bets someone at his New York club that he can break into any house as Raffles does. He chooses, by accident, the house of a crooked New York policeman, John McEachern, an Englishman called Forest who took on an Irish moniker and made a successful career in the New York police force by corrupt means.

But Wodehouse is at pains to point out that McEachern is merely working his way through a corrupt system. McEachern is not censured by the author from taking a cut of the criminal activity of those whose actions he is supposed to curtail. He did not invent the system, he merely works it. He wants money so as to re-establish himself in English society through his daughter, whom he wants to marry into it. He is, however, made to repent, and to confess his deeds to the daughter he loves and worships, and who returns this affection. He finishes the book having achieved his aim of getting deeply embedded into the society of his homeland. He had a place in this originally, through birth, but forfeited it by getting expelled from Eton for stealing. The satirist in Wodehouse then shipped this thief off to America to become a successful policeman, a success built on physical strength and bribery.

The book closes with Spike Mullins, a burglar who is not inclined to forego his criminal intentions, setting sail back to his homeland of America. But he is to abandon his career of housebreaker in favour of one in politics. Jimmy Pitt foresees that he will become 'a thundering success' in this new career as he has 'all the necessary qualities.'

Wodehouse sees the true corruption not in the policeman on the make but in the politicians who run a crooked political system. Crooks are allowed to flourish because of the favours they do for the politicians. It was an argument he was to develop in *Psmith, Journalist*. Here the author explains why criminal gangs are happily tolerated by the lawmakers:

> The New York gangs, and especially the Groome Street gang, have brought to a fine art the gentle practice of 'repeating', which, broadly speaking, is the art of voting a number of different times at different polling stations on election days. A man who can vote, say, ten times in a single day for you, and who controls a great number of followers who are also prepared, if they like you, to vote ten times in a single day for you, is worth cultivating. So the politicians passed the word to the police, and the police left the Groome Street gang unmolested and they waxed and flourished.

Psmith is investigating a politician called Waring, who used to be Commissioner for Buildings:

> 'What exactly did that let him in for?'
> 'It let him in for a lot of graft.'
> 'How was that?'
> 'Oh, he took it off the contractors. Shut his eyes and held out his hands when they ran up rotten buildings that a strong breeze would have knocked down, and places like that Pleasant Street hole without any ventilation.'
> 'Why did he throw up the job?'

'His trouble was that he stood in with a contractor who was putting up a music hall, and the contractor put it up with material about as strong as a heap of meringues, and it collapsed on the third night and killed half the audience.'

McEachern is a keen disciple of the practice of 'grafting'. He grafts so as to earn the money to buy his next promotion. Though he did not like having to pay this money, he saw it as an investment, and knew that to accumulate he had to speculate. Each stage further up the ladder increases the opportunity to accept bribes.

McEachern is the first of many Englishmen who find that America transforms them either materially or personally. Freddie Threepwood moves to America and is transformed from a useless drone to a go-getting businessman. Once looked down upon by his father, Lord Emsworth, for being nothing but a wastrel, Freddie now looks down upon his father for his lack of get up and go. Lord Ickenham is also married to an American and credits America with the making of him, and presumes that it will do the same for Pongo. In the world Wodehouse was to carve out in his books America is where the money is, and England is where social standing is to be obtained. Many of his plots were about the marrying of the two.

It is in search of social respectability that McEachern comes over to Dreever Castle, with his daughter whom he hopes will marry the 12th Earl of Dreever. It would be a loveless marriage, based on her money and his title. The plan fails as young love wins through, each party marrying the one they love instead.

Many of the features which were to become part of a typical Wodehouse novel had been assembled in *A Gentleman Of Leisure*: opening scene is in a club; hero is a good boxer; an unexpected inheritance; a private detective masquerades as a valet; love at first sight is followed by the briefest of courtships; young love triumphs over the machinations of the older generation; English and American characters mix together on both sides of the Atlantic; coincidences which strain at the bounds of believability; the theft of a necklace; unflattering portraits of members of the aristocracy; English scenes are set at a stately home; America is shown to be where the money is and England is where people head for when they want to turn this money into something less tangible to do with class.

The novel also takes a few strides towards comedy. At this stage Wodehouse was still reluctant to give in to his natural desire to aim for comedy, but the character Spike Mullins is there for comic interludes. The hero, Jimmy Pitt, has traces of Psmith: he is self-confident, at ease with words and determined. He has a hardness when it comes to ensuring that he will be alright which Psmith also possesses. The best of Wodehouse's early heroes were to have traces of Psmith in them in respect of their coolness and love of words. In time, though, the hardness of these characters was to dissipate.

A Gentleman Of Leisure is thus recognisable as a 'typical Wodehouse product'. It was not to be long before he re-used the template he had formed with this book. This was *Something Fresh*, the first of the Blandings series.

At this early stage of his career Wodehouse was reluctant to speak with his own voice. Later, when he was more successful and so more assured of his place, he was to sculpt a style of writing that was highly individual; he was also to be increasingly a comic novelist. But at this stage of his career Wodehouse was a 'slanter'. Writing an introduction for a new edition of *The Man With Two Left Feet*, a collection of 13 short stories which was originally published in 1917, a 90-year old Wodehouse reflected:

> There seems to me now something synthetic about them, and there probably was, for when I wrote them I had become a slanter. A slanter is a writer who studies what editors want. He reads magazines carefully and turns out stories as like the ones they

are publishing as he can manage without actual plagiarism. It is a deadly practice.

Shortly after my arrival in New York an editor who had apparently seen signs of promise in the little thing of mine he was rejecting told me he thought I would eventually amount to something. 'But,' he added, 'don't try to write like everyone else.'

I did not take his advice. I knew better... I was mistaken.

The other short-story collection to be published in this period was *The Man Upstairs*. They include *The Good Angel*, which gives a leading role to a butler, and another where a girl conducts a feud with a policeman, and asks her fiancé to pull the copper's helmet down over his eyes, an idea he was to recycle for Stiffy Byng in *The Code Of The Woosters*. *The Romance Of An Ugly Policeman* features a husband whose wife controls the purse strings. But they are an odd collection when viewed from the distance of a modern reader. In subject matter alone these collections would not be immediately recognisable as a Wodehouse product. They are about the struggles of the petit bourgeois. They are about some of the types of people Wodehouse moved among, people struggling to make their way in life. Indeed, *In Alcala*, Wodehouse weaves details of his own life into his portrait of Rutherford Maxwell:

Rutherford Maxwell was an Englishman and the younger son of an Englishman; and his lot was the lot of the younger sons all the world over. He was by profession one of the numerous employees of the New Asiatic Bank, which has its branches all over the world. It is a sound, trustworthy institution, and steady-going relatives would assure Rutherford that he was lucky to have a berth in it. Rutherford did not agree with them. However sound and trustworthy, it was not exactly romantic. Nor did it err on the side of over-lavishness to those who served it. Rutherford's salary was small. So were his prospects - if he remained in the bank. At a very early date he had registered a vow that he would not. And the road that led out of it for him was the uphill road of literature. He was thankful for small mercies. Fate had not been over-kind up to the present, but at least she had dispatched him to New York, the centre of things, where he would have the chance to try, instead of to some spot off the map. Whether he won or lost, at any rate he was in the ring, and could fight. So every night he sat in Alcala, and wrote. Sometimes he would only try to write, and that was torture.

If you picked up this book by an author who you had only met through, say, *Mike, The Code Of The Woosters* or *Heavy Weather*, you would be surprised. It is a sombre collection. It is Wodehouse trying to be an American writer, doing what American writers did. When he decided to be an English author, writing what Americans might expect an Englishman to write about, he was more successful and wrote much better work.

Wodehouse did not, as at least one commentator has hinted, 'improve' himself, then try to bury his past, and start writing about the activities of earls and their butlers because that was the society into which his financial rewards from writing had propelled him. Wodehouse started married life without any domestic staff, but by the mid-thirties his retinue ran to butler, footman, cook, two housemaids, a parlour maid, a scullery maid and a chauffeur who drove the Rolls. Wodehouse was born into the upper-middle class, and was never a member of the struggling petit bourgeoisie. His struggles consisted of a failure to get to university and to persuade his father that he could make a career as a freelance writer; he had a respected and decently paid job in a bank while earning an equally respectable income from his extra-curricular activities while receiving an allowance from his father of a sum greater than some families' income. These are not the typical struggles of the petit bourgeoisie. Wodehouse was born of high social standing, and did not rise through the social strata through his writing. All he did was rise though the financial pecking order.

Wodehouse turned to writing about the English upper classes as a result of his geographical situation. What, he realised, the American public wanted from him was not pastiches of work they were already receiving in abundance from their home-grown writers but something different, something fresh even. So Wodehouse instead started writing stories of a section of English society that the Americans did not have - aristocracy. *A Gentleman Of Leisure* had been a success in America, and was turned into a play of the same name by Wodehouse in collaboration with John Stapleton and ran for 76 performances at The Playhouse in New York in the autumn of 1911, and gave a first starring role to Douglas Fairbanks. Later, renamed *A Thief For A Night*, it was performed in Chicago, where John Barrymore played the lead.

But the aim of any writer was publication in the *Saturday Evening Post*. The editor of this journal was George Horace Lorimer and he was to be a leading influence on Wodehouse's career. Lorimer was an editor with a message. He set about creating, through the pages of his magazine, a vision of the America he wanted, one proud of its past achievements and positive as to its commercial future. The magazine's editorial character reflected its editor's vision. He wanted stories in praise of business success, romantic stories and tales about public matters. These categories could be mixed together. Thus a romance story entwined with the demonstration of the virtues of good business sense would fit the bill nicely.

Lorimer was the son of a preacher who was busy with a large debt-ridden Walnut Street Baptist Church. His father turned around the church's finances. After spending a year at Yale University, Lorimer left to go into business in the meat-packing firm of one of his father's parishioners. Within five years Lorimer was head of the canning department, but he canned the job to go Colby College in Maine. During the last years of the 19th century he worked on several Boston newspapers before he got a job as literary editor of the *Saturday Evening Post*, which, bankrupt, had been acquired by Cyrus Curtis in 1897. In 1899 the editor left and Lorimer took over on, initially, a temporary basis while a more qualified candidate was sought.

Lorimer rapidly transformed the financial fortunes of the *Post*. His vision of America made the magazine popular with the young, aspiring middle classes. He aimed to entertain first, but he also sought to challenge his readership. He admired hard work and men of business. His *Letters Of A Self Made Man To His Son* was a humorous series with the serious purpose of preparing young men to be a success in business - as Lorimer was. When Curtis had bought the *SEP* in 1897 circulation was 2,000; three years after Lorimer took over it had risen to 350,000. By 1908 it had reached 1 million, and it had doubled to 2 million by 1919; when Lorimer retired in 1936 its circulation stood at 3 million.

Under Lorimer's encouragement and guidance Wodehouse's career blossomed. Lorimer required high standards for his writers, and paid accordingly. He read each submission on the quality of the work not the power of the name. He had no need for big names, the *Saturday Evening Post* was always going to be biggest name in his magazine. If the *Post* published you, you were good, was his simple philosophy. Thus he had no need of name writers, nor of commissioning work: there were always plenty of people eagerly submitting manuscripts.

Partly through Lorimer's influence, the standard Wodehouse hero became established as a young man of spirit, eager to progress through hard work. Many of these characters would be reformed drones, who gave up a life sponging off the family name or money to strike out for themselves.

Piccadilly Jim, the third novel which Wodehouse sold to the *SEP* for serialisation, was a very Lorimer-friendly work. There is a successful businessman, Peter Pett, of whom it was written:

> It was the tapping of the typewriter that he heard, and he listened to it with an air of benevolent approval. He loved to hear the sound of a typewriter; it made home so like the office.

Jimmy Crocker becomes a reformed drone after he decides that leading a wild life by spending his inheritance is not the way to fulfilment and happiness and that the route to this instead involves joining Mr Pett's firm and carving out a career in business. Willie Partridge, also previously content to live off his father's achievements, follows Jimmy into Mr Pett's company. This book is in the adventure story tradition of Wodehouse's early works as it includes kidnap, burglary, gun play, explosives and the secret service.

Something Fresh is the poorest of the Blandings saga. Indeed, it was not conceived as part of a series, which really began with another book which was not set at Blandings. The best part by far is the introduction of Lord Emsworth, which happens in a club, and the long scene he plays with the waiter, Adams, of which this is the finest section:

> 'Tell me, Adams, have I eaten my cheese?'
> 'Not yet, your lordship. I was about to send the waiter for it.'
> 'Never mind. Tell him to bring the bill instead. I remember that I have an appointment. I must not be late.'
> 'Shall I take the fork your lordship?'
> 'The fork?'
> 'Your lordship has inadvertently put a fork in your coat-pocket.'

Lord Emsworth felt in the pocket indicated, and, with the air of an inexpert conjuror whose trick has succeeded contrary to his expectations, produced a silver-plated fork.

This episode is also notable as being the first of only two funny scenes in the book. It is a stodgy work. At this stage of his career Wodehouse had a tendency to write long introductions to his chapters, often going on for paragraph after paragraph. The ratio of dialogue to description was to increase as the books progressed. Wodehouse upped the dialogue of his books as his theatrical influences deepened.

At this stage of his career it was the stage where he had most success. At one time there were five shows running on Broadway for which Wodehouse had written. As Wodehouse was also dramatic critic of *Vanity Fair*, he was an important figure in the world of New York theatre. Indeed, he often ended up reviewing his own shows. Wodehouse's success in the theatre and the role he played in the development of the musical is largely ignored by modern readers and commentators. I intend to do the same, except in so far as it influenced his novel-writing.

Wodehouse's most successful period in musical comedy was when he teamed up with Guy Bolton and Jerome Kern. Guy Bolton, a short, dapper man whom Gally Threepwood was to take after in appearance, became a close and lifelong friend and his working relationship with Wodehouse lasted long after their collaboration with the temperamental Kern, who wrote the music, had ended. Bolton and Wodehouse looked after the words; the book was normally Bolton's main concern while Wodehouse busied himself with the lyrics.

Wodehouse could not read music, so he would listen to the tune, write a dummy lyric based on the rhythm, and then write a proper lyric to fit this. He claimed that knowing the music in advance meant he knew where the stresses of various words had to go. As ever, he preferred having something to work from. He needed that template.

The musicals the trio put on at the Princess Theatre nudged the musical theatre towards a more modern phase. A typical musical of that period was a foreign import, with a huge cast, ever-changing sets, glittering costumes, and improbable and disjointed plots which were suspended while the musical numbers were played out. Wodehouse disliked this type of piece:

> The plot of *The Girl From Brighton* had by then reached a critical stage. The situation was as follows: the hero, having been disinherited by his wealthy and titled father for falling in love with the heroine, a poor shop-girl, has disguised himself (by wearing a different-coloured necktie), and has come in pursuit of her to a well-known seaside resort, where, having disguised herself by changing her dress, she is serving as a waitress in the Rotunda, on the Esplanade. The family butler, disguised as a Bath-chair man, has followed the hero, and the wealthy and titled father, disguised as an Italian opera singer, has come to the place for a reason which, though entirely sound, for the moment eludes the memory. Anyhow, he is there, and they all meet on the Esplanade. Each recognises the other, but thinks himself is unrecognised. Exeunt all, hurriedly, leaving the heroine alone on stage. It is a crisis in the heroine's life. She meets it bravely. She sings a song entitled 'My Honolulu Queen', with a chorus of Japanese girls and Bulgarian officers. [*Bill The Bloodhound*]

In passing it might be noted that by wearing a different-coloured necktie at least the impostor has shown more imagination than many of Wodehouse's charlatans. Psmith, for example, masquerades as a Canadian poet without bothering to adopt a Canadian accent, nor find out about his life and work. In a Wodehouse novel, all an impostor needs to do is change his name and that will be disguise enough.

The Princess Theatre could only hold 299, which was a deliberate policy as the fire regulations only applied to auditoria of at least 300 seats. However the limit on the audience numbers restricted the production budget. Princess shows had to have a small cast and orchestra and no more than two sets. Thus was born a new type of musical: an intimate show written with comedy and a strong narrative where the song lyrics were designed to move the plot on.

Wodehouse was involved with 51 dramatic works, either through writing the lyrics or book, or bits of both for musicals, or from collaborating with others on adaptations, either of his own works or others. Although Wodehouse is now viewed, perhaps unfairly, as a novelist who dabbled in the theatre; had he died in, say, 1920, the obituaries would have been about a lyricist not a novelist.

It is impossible to separate Wodehouse's theatre work from a critical look at his novels for the skills learnt in one field were transferred to another. Extracts from *Performing Flea* show how Wodehouse did this:

> I believe there are two ways of writing novels. One is mine, making the thing a sort of musical comedy without music, and ignoring real life altogether; the other is going right deep down into life and not caring a damn.
>
> In writing a novel, I always imagine I am writing for a cast of actors. Some actors are natural minor actors and some are natural major ones. It is a matter of personality. Same in a book. Psmith, for instance, is a major character. If I am going to have Psmith in a story, it must be in the big situations.

This philosophy lead to Baxter being given the flowerpot scene in *Leave It To Psmith*. Wodehouse realised that Baxter's was a more major part than the draft plot had allowed for, so he wrote this scene to boost his part. Sometimes, though, Wodehouse could fail to follow his own advice. Spode is given only a small role in *Jeeves And The Feudal Spirit*. A major character in *The Code Of The Woosters*, he is wasted here.

Wodehouse's work for the theatre also taught him the importance of dialogue and action. As he began to find his own voice as a novelist, he moved away from some of the introspective writing, where he would, often rather cack-handedly, describe what his characters were thinking. His theatrical influence told him that you had to deduce what a character thought by how he acted and what he said so his novels increasingly came to be mainly dialogue. However he preferred writing novels to playwriting because novels allowed him to write some author narrative. It is these passages which raise his work as a novelist above his work as a playwright. But it was the playwright in him which made them increasingly pithy and concise, rather than the rather rambling reams of paragraphs he could sometimes stumble into when not on prime form. Part of Bertie Wooster's memorability as a character is his summations of characters and situations. The Wooster line 'she fitted into my largest armchair as if it had been built round her by someone who knew they were wearing armchairs tight rounds the hips this season' [*Jeeves And The Unbidden Guest*], would become merely a stage direction in a play.

Wodehouse began to structure his novels as a series of scenes. Sometimes the playwright influence becomes very evident when, for instance, something exciting happens off stage and is only told to the reader in reported speech. Though this is often necessary in a play, where only a limited number of scenes and settings are possible, a novelist can go where he wants and watch what he wants. Wodehouse could sometimes be reluctant to take this opportunity. A blatant example of this technique is in *The Old Reliable* in which virtually all the action takes place in the Garden Room and any action which happens anywhere else is reported. *The Old Reliable* is based upon a play and Wodehouse persists in treating his readers just as if they were a play audience. Thus, when a drunken butler fails to carry out a safe-blow, which has the makings of a big comic scene, we do not see it, but merely get a brief résumé of what happens from a character who enters the Garden Room and tells the players there what has been happening.

Something Fresh, although a disappointing work when viewed alongside what was to come from Blandings Castle, established Wodehouse a notch higher up the scale as a novelist on its acceptance by the *Saturday Evening Post*, and its fee of $3,500 was far more than any work had previously brought him. However, few of the characters in the book have any marked personality. Lord Emsworth makes a brilliant entrance, but he fades away from then on. Indeed, it could be argued that the best prolonged piece of writing about Lord Emsworth is the first scene Wodehouse wrote for him, and that nothing reached this level during the following six decades.

One of the best books Wodehouse wrote, and one often overlooked, is *A Damsel In Distress*, which came out four years after *Something Fresh*. It is notable in two main ways. The first is that it contains an oddity in Wodehouse literature in that the scene between Maud and George Bevan on the terrace is atmospheric and serious. The quality of the writing is not unusual; that Wodehouse should produce such a fine piece of writing from the type of scene he normally stumbles through is. Wodehouse recognised his strengths and weaknesses and was to shun this type of scene later on. But here he shows that he could pull it off.

The main significance of the novel, however, is that it sets the template for the Blandings saga. It is not, as has been claimed, that *A Damsel In Distress* copies the Blandings books, but the opposite. *A Damsel In Distress* is set at Belpher Castle, the seat of Lord Marshmoreton. His lordship is a more rounded character and gets a much fatter part than Lord Emsworth in *Something Fresh*. A widower, he is bullied by his sister and his family, but he does retain some of his old character, which resurfaces when he defies the family and allows his daughter Maud to marry into musical theatre, in the form of the wealthy composer George Bevan. Previously he had been keen to forbid the marriage, even though he liked George, so as to preserve a quiet life for himself, as the union is opposed by his sister and son. Yet Lord Marshmoreton's change of mind is not motivated by the nobility of his character but from self-interest, as he himself marries a girl from the chorus.

Marriage in Wodehouse normally equals retirement and so this is the last we see of his lordship. When Wodehouse came to plot his fourth novel to be set at a country house, rather than invent a fourth country house he reverted to Blandings Castle. The Lord Emsworth of the second Blandings Castle is different from the one in the first. Like Lord Marshmoreton, in the first novel he is a keen gardener and a widower. Unlike Lord Marshmoreton, he was not bullied by a sister. The sister who plays hostess in *Something Fresh* is Lady Ann Warblington, a quiet character given to headaches and avoiding her guests by staying in her room either feeling unwell or writing letters. She is never to appear again in the Blandings chronicles; in her place come a succession of fierce sisters to bully Lord Emsworth and obstruct the path of young love. Lady Constance was run off from the template established with the creation of the snobbish Lady Caroline of Belpher Castle. Despite *Something Fresh* involving the descent of Lord Emsworth's relatives upon Blandings to mark Freddie's engagement, there are no sisters mentioned other than the feeble Lady Ann. Belpher Castle has set up camp at Blandings Castle.

Blandings Castle is not brought out again to provide a Blandings story as such, but to provide a backdrop for Psmith's manoeuvres. Indeed, the Blandings series of books are a mix of the self-sufficient, where the family provide the characters and the plot, and those where the facilities of the castle are hired out to others. Psmith has a novel set there, and Lord Ickenham two. When Lord Ickenham first invades the castle, Lord Emsworth is almost booted off stage, so small a part does he get, and Gally does not make it onto the cast list at all and neither does he feature when Lord Ickehnam returns to the castle in *Service With A Smile*. Wodehouse also planned to set a Wooster novel there, but could not settle on the exact plot or treatment. Blandings will provide the supporting cast, but the leads are normally brought in from outside. Only two characters are common to all the Blandings stories: Lord Emsworth and Beach. Gally and the Empress of Blandings first make their appearances in the third novel of the series.

During the writing of *Something Fresh* Wodehouse had become a married man. Like the characters in his books, the courtship was brief and the marriage ceremony a simple one. His bride was a widow twice over, with a daughter from her first marriage. This showed a consistency of choice, for Wodehouse had already had one proposal of marriage turned down by another widow with a daughter.

On 3 August 1914 Ethel Rowley first met her third husband-to-be when she was asked by a girlfriend to make up a fourth in a party which included two men. Wodehouse was the second man and he proposed to her within days and they were married on 30 September. He was to remain married for the rest of his life, as he predeceased his wife after 60 years together.

Many of his works written when he was single talked of loneliness in a way that suggests it was a personal experience:

New York is a better city than London to be alone in, but it is never pleasant to be alone in a big city. [*Psmith, Journalist*]

He wrote to a friend after his marriage saying that for the first time he was happy. This letter slightly questions the traditional view of his time at Dulwich, which it was generally considered that he enjoyed. Perhaps it merely suggests that the happiness of his Dulwich schooldays was by then a distant memory.

What Ethel was doing in America has generally been ignored by biographers. However it seems that she was on the stage there, in the chorus. One of the stock Wodehouse heroines is a girl who has taken to the stage to provide for herself. In the case of Ethel, it would to be provide for herself and her daughter, left behind in England in the care of her grandparents. Ethel was of the lower middle classes, the daughter of a farmer. She professed to hate her mother, who she said was an alcoholic, and was mainly brought up by her grandmother on her father's side.

The picture which has been allowed to develop is of Ethel as a dominating, bossy woman and Wodehouse an unworldly recluse happy to let his wife cope with the everyday details of life which he found so daunting. Stories which back up this point of view include the one in which, when Ethel was about to set off to find a flat for them to live in, her husband made a plaintive plea that she find one on the ground floor as he could never think of anything to say to the lift attendant. This picture of the Wodehouse version of domestic bliss suited both of them. Malcolm Muggeridge, who got to know the Wodehouses well and liked them both, wrote of Ethel Wodehouse as being 'A high-spirited and energetic lady trying as hard to be as worldly wise as Wodehouse himself to be innocent.' [*Chronicles of Wasted Time*]. Ethel Wodehouse was gregarious and a keen hostess. This contrasted with her husband who preferred human conduct to be on a one-to-one basis. One of the advantages of this was that he could control the subject matter of the conversation in a way not possible with a group. Wodehouse's favourite topic of conversation was writing, both his own and others. He was equally as avid a reader as writer. Not only was he a prolific writer in a professional sense, he was also a keen correspondent. Many of those to whom he would write regularly he might not have seen for years, decades even. Some he had not met.

Ethel was not the dictator she has often been painted as. The family's life was based around Plum. They moved around the world according to what suited him best for his career, which was the dominating force of their life. The organisation of their day-to-day existence he was happy to leave to Ethel. She organised and ran the household, and would set about alterations to the decor - or sometimes even the whole building - of the places they lived in, while he was left to get on with his writing. Increasingly their lifestyle came to be rooted in his interests and work rather than in her preferences and tastes.

Wodehouse was a man happy in his own company or, perhaps that should be, happy in the company of a typewriter. Wodehouse made few really close friends, though he was liked by many. The closest of his friends was Ethel. Theirs appears to be a marriage based on comfort and companionship. Writing to a friend shortly after his marriage, Wodehouse argued that marriage was not so much about love as finding someone with whom you shared enough points in common to enable you to live happily together without getting on each other's nerves. It is believed that Wodehouse's bout of mumps meant he was never going to have children himself, but he adored his step-daughter, Leonora, and was devastated when she died in 1944, aged 40, after a routine operation.

As everything for Wodehouse fed into, or was centred on, his writing, where did his close family fit in? Ethel it is said is the role model for Lady Constance Keeble with Lord Emsworth playing the PG Wodehouse role, happy to be left alone with his own preoccupations, while the dominant female in his life forces him into taking an interest in outside matters and to dress up and be sociable.

Ethel is also cited as a possible influence in the creation of the Wooster aunt. But is it too fanciful to say that it might not be to Agatha that attention should be turned, but to Aunt

Julia, whose only appearance is in the first Bertie story, where faint traces of Ethel's situation may be found:

> Nobody ever mentions it, and the family have been trying to forget it for twenty-five years, but it's a known fact that my Aunt Julia, Gussie's mother, was a vaudeville artist once, and very good one, too, I'm told. She was playing in pantomime at Drury Lane when Uncle Cuthbert saw her first. It was before my time, of course, and long before I was old enough to take notice the family had made the best of it, and Aunt Agatha had put in a lot of educative work and with a microscope you couldn't tell Aunt Julia from a genuine dyed-in-the-wool aristocrat. Women adapt themselves so quickly!

Leonora's influence can be seen in the fact that, after Wodehouse had met her, his female heroines because more robust, rounded characters. Frances Donaldson, a family friend and a Wodehouse biographer, claimed that every heroine looked like his step-daughter. Leonora became a published author herself, under the name Leol Yeo, and Wodehouse came to rely upon her judgement and, whenever possible, would to get her to read his completed manuscripts before they were submitted to publishers.

Wodehouse loved to write anything and everything. He had success on Broadway both in musicals and straight theatre, and by the 1930s he was an accomplished and successful novelist and short-story writer. Keen to try his hand at anything within his compass in the writing field, he set out for Hollywood to write screenplays. In the autumn of 1929 he visited Hollywood, having had, like every other successful writer of the time, approaches to work as a screenwriter there. He spent three days there, liked what he saw and expected to take up a contract to work there from the next summer following three offers of a year's work. Wodehouse originally turned down an offer to work for MGM as the money was not good enough, but in May 1930 he arrived in Hollywood, having agreed to a six-month contract with MGM at $2,000 a week, with an option of a further six months.

As a screenwriter his career is almost entirely forgettable. Mainly because he thought the studio who had hired him had forgotten about him. Used to hard and intensive work, Wodehouse found the studio had little for him to do. On those projects he got to work on, he was only one of a team of writers, with no guarantee that the screenplay would ever be shot. Many were not and the trade journal *Variety* made pointed comments about an 'English playwright and author who has been collecting $2,500 a week for eleven months without contributing anything really worthwhile to the screen.' The figure was wrong, but there was no doubt that it was to Wodehouse that they referred.

MGM did not renew his contract and in June Wodehouse gave an interview to Alma Whitaker of the *Los Angeles Times* at MGM's request. She opened her piece with some casual remarks Wodehouse had made before the interview had begun:

'They paid me $2,000 a week, - $104,000 - and I cannot see what they engaged me for,' he said wonderingly as we sat beneath the coconut palms beside his glistening swimming pool in Benedict Canyon. 'The motion picture business dazes me. They were extremely nice to me - oh, extremely - but I feel as if I cheated them. It's all so unreasonable.

'You see, I understood I was engaged to write stories for the screen. After all, I have twenty novels, a score of successful plays, and countless magazine stories to my credit.

'Yet apparently they had the greatest difficulty in finding anything for me to do. Twice during the year they brought completed scenarios of other people's stories to me and asked me to do some dialogue. Fifteen or sixteen people had tinkered with these stories. The dialogue was really quite adequate. All I did was touch it up here and there - very slight improvements.

Then they set me to work on a story called *Rosalie* which was to have some musical numbers. No, it wasn't my story. But it was a pleasant little thing, and I put in three months' work on it. No one wanted me to hurry. When it was finished they thanked me politely and remarked that as musicals didn't seem to be going so well they would not use it. That about sums up what I was called upon to do for my $104,000.'

According to legend, this interview rocked Hollywood and caused the financiers to descend upon Tinsletown and pore through the books demanding swingeing cuts to the budget and rationalisations in the way the place worked. In fact, though the interview did cause ripples, its effect was less marked. Some of the film papers ignored the interview altogether, though the *New York Herald Tribune* carried an editorial on the subject. The myth of the interview was partly created by Wodehouse himself as part of 'his silly old me, look what a fool I've been now' act. He was often the butt of his own jokes, but rarely of anyone else's. He was not the simpleton he often liked to make out he was. The imagined repercussions of his interview made a good story and Wodehouse always liked a good story.

Far from becoming a moral leper at Hollywood, he received further offers of work, turning them down because at the time he was in conflict with the American tax authorities and was doubtful of how much of his salary he would ever see. He eventually returned in 1936 for a six-month stint with MGM and after that worked on some films on a single-picture only basis. When he returned in 1936, the first project he was given to work on was *Rosalie* which was an old - and regular - acquaintance by then, as he had also worked on the original Broadway version.

Hollywood, though giving him little in the way of screenwriting, was to give him inspiration in his other work. When an American magazine commissioned him to write six stories with the proviso that they were about Americans in American settings, he set to work on stories about Hollywood. These are the most satirical of his work once he had become established as an author. In *The Castaways*, Jacob Z. Schnellenhamer, President of the Perfecto-Zizzbaum Picture Corp, has taken Bulstrode Mulliner's hat by mistake and Bulstrode goes to retrieve it:

The motion-picture magnate took a quick look at Bulstrode and thrust a paper and a fountain pen towards him.

'Sign here,' he said.

A receipt for the hat, no doubt, thought Bulstrode. He scribbled his name at the bottom of the document and Mr Schnellenhamer pressed the bell.

'Miss Stern,' he said, addressing his secretary, 'what vacant offices have we on the lot?'

'There is Room 40 in the Leper Colony.'

'I thought there was a song-writer there.'

'He passed away last Tuesday.'

'Has the body been removed?'

'Yes, sir.'

Then Mr Mulliner will occupy the room, starting from to-day. He has just signed a contract to write dialogue for us.'

Bulstrode would have spoken, but Mr Schnellenhamer silenced him with a gesture.

'Who are working on 'Scented Sinners' now?' he asked.

The secretary consulted a list.

Mr Doakes, Mr Noakes, Miss Faversham, Miss Wilson, Mr Fotheringay, Mr Mendelson, Mr Murkey, Mrs Cooper, Mr Lennox and Mr Dabney.'

'That all?'

'There was a missionary who came in Thursday, wanting to convert the extra girls. He started a treatment, but he has escaped to Canada.

'Tcah!' said Schnellenhamer, annoyed. 'We must have more vigilance, more vigilance. Give Mr Mulliner a script of 'Scented Sinners' before he goes.'

Other aspects of Hollywood were sent up by Wodehouse. That the moguls were greatly interested in money but not in literature or the English language is a point many of Hollywood's commentators and satirists have noted. Producing quotes by Samuel Goldwyn, famous for his inability with the English language, became a veritable cottage industry, with comments such as 'a verbal contract isn't worth the paper it's written on'. Goldwyn reportedly demanded that Shakespeare be sent for to tidy up the dialogue in Othello, and in *The Luck Of The Bodkins* Ambrose Tennyson is to work for Superba-Llewellyn, as its chief, Ivor Llewellyn, thinks he is the famous writer Tennyson he has heard about.

In *The Juice of An Orange*, Mr Schnellenhamer is in conference with his fellow magnate, Mr Levitsky:

'Every time I said anything, its seemed to me that he did something funny with the side of his mouth. Drew it up in a twisted way that looked kind of... what's that word beginning with an 's'?'

'Cynical?'

'No, a snickle is a thing you cut corn with. Ah, I've got it, sardinic. Every time I spoke he looked sardinic.'

Mr Levitsky was out of his depth.

'Like a sardine, do you mean?'

Studio chiefs, as well as being ignorant of the finer points of world literature, and often the blunter points as well, were often generous toward their families when drawing up the company pay rolls. Harry Cohn found a place for twenty-nine of his relatives on the pay roll of Columbia when he was its chief. Willmot Mulliner finds himself promoted to executive status 'with brevet rank as brother-in-law.'

What Wodehouse was doing in Hollywood the second time around is hard to say. He had one try at it, found little to do, and had not greatly enjoyed that which he did do. The second time around he wrote to a friend saying how he hated screenwriting. Guy Bolton made the point that Wodehouse struggled to appreciate the fact that the camera could follow the characters around. Wodehouse was too stuck on the theatrical concept of there being one set, whereby when a character walks out of a room you can no longer see them. This makes sense as criticism, as it applies to his novels as well, so one would expect to find it hindering his screenplay work, where the construction is closer to that of a theatrical piece.

But just as those mountaineers who know of a large mountain and decide they have to climb it 'as it is there', so Wodehouse, a professional writer, had to try Hollywood simply because it was there. He was well paid for being there, Ethel had a fine time as a hostess, and Wodehouse got plots and ideas for novels and short stories. Also, he got one of the best lines in all his work in the Hollywood story, *Monkey Business*, when it is decided that a gorilla will be allowed to escape so as to garner publicity for a forthcoming film.

> 'The stars have all been notified and are off the lot. Also the executives, all except Mr Schnellenhamer, who is clearing up some work in his office. He will be quite safe there, of course. Nobody ever got into Mr Schellenhamer's office without waiting four hours in the ante room.

Treatment

What is plagiarism? Did you ever see a play by Freddie Lonsdale called The Last of Mrs Cheyney? It was about a society woman who was one of a band of crooks, and this is revealed to the audience at the end of Act I. An exactly similar situation was in an American play called Cheating Cheaters. And the big scene in Act II was where the hero gets Mrs Cheyney into his room at night and holds her up for something by saying he is going to keep her there till they are found in the morning, which is exactly the same as Pinero's Gay Lord Quex. And yet nobody has ever breathed a word against Freddie for plagiarising. Quite rightly. The treatment is everything. [*Performing Flea*]

Wodehouse was to be plagued by plots throughout his writing life. The actual technique of writing held no perils for him. He could write quickly and felicitously. What he had to have, though, was something to write about. When he worked on a daily column for *The Globe* that was no problem, for that day's news gave him something to bounce off. But the blank piece of paper held a terror for him if he was not sure of the structure of the piece that was to fill it. With that firmly fixed, he could write rapidly and without anxiety. In the many letters in *Performing Flea* never once does he complain of difficulties with the art of writing, though he did complain as he got older that he could not write so quickly. What he is always complaining of is the difficulty of getting plots. One method was simple plagiarism, as the full text of two letters which appear in abridged form in *Performing Flea* illustrate. These extracts were cut out when the letters were edited for publication:

> I have got a new system for writing short stories. I take a *Saturday Evening Post* story and say, 'Now, how can I write exactly the same story but entirely different?' ... I have faith in the method. It at least does this - it sets one thinking, - and then some other plot on quite different lines emerges. [letter, 2 December 1935 to William Townend]
> I find nowadays that the only way I can get plots is by reading somebody else's stuff and working from there. I was reading a book the other day, called No Hero, where the fatal paper is hidden in a man's flask, and the man, who has always been a ready drinker, suddenly decides to reform and so does not touch the flask. If I can't get something out of that, I'm not the man I was.
> I don't think there is any objection to basing one's stuff on somebody else's, providing you alter it enough. After all, all one wants is motives. [letter, 6 May 1937, to William Townend]

The idea of the flask came into use in *Money In The Bank*. Wodehouse adapted the idea into the tobacco jar of a man who has given up smoking, and the item becomes some diamonds which Lord Uffenham wants as a dowry for his niece. The plot for *Money In the Bank* shows how Wodehouse would filter both his reading and real life experiences into his work. Lord Uffenham is a large, pear-shaped man with huge feet and a tendency to go into trances and impart strange bits of information unrelated to anything which might be going on around him. Wodehouse based this character on Max Enke, a man he knew in prison camp. Lord Uffenham has had to rent out his ancestral home, but he stays on in the guise of butler, hoping his memory of where he hid the diamonds will come back to him. The house, Shipley Hall, is based on Fairlawne, in Shipbourne, Kent, where Wodehouse's step-daughter lived. It was not the first time this location had popped up in Wodehouse's fictional world. In *All's Well For Bingo*, a short story which, at that time, Wodehouse thought was the best he had yet written, Bingo Little is despatched by his novelist wife Rosie M. Banks to Monte Carlo to collect local colour for one her books, the hero of whom is Lord Peter Shipbourne. Wodehouse's son-in-law was called Peter.

Wodehouse liked these in-jokes. In *Sticky Wicket At Blandings*, Lord Emsworth misremembers his daughter-in-law's name as Frances Donaldson rather than Aggie Donaldson. Frances Donaldson was a friend of Wodehouse's step-daughter, and later became his biographer. In *Barmy In Wonderland*, a court case is cited, Schwed versus Meredith. Wodehouse's American publisher's representative was Peter Schwed, and his American agent was Scott Meredith. In *Big Business*, Reginald Mulliner gets a letter from the solicitors Watson, Watson, Watson, Watson and Watson. Wodehouse's American attorney at that time was Watson Washburn.

Shipley Hall in *Money In the Bank* is being run as a vegetarian, teetotal health establishment. This idea may well have come to Wodehouse through the obsession with food and straitened diet he and his fellow prisoners had to cope with.

Wodehouse would frequently gain inspiration from events in his own life. The plot for *Money For Nothing* centred on a fake burglary and was written a few months after Wodehouse's Norfolk Street house had been burgled. In 1920 a conman tried to interest Wodehouse in shares in a dud gold mine. Wodehouse declined his invitation, but five years later came the publication of *Sam The Sudden* and the first appearance of Thomas 'Soapy' Molloy, an enthusiastic salesman of duff oil stock.

The solution to the mystery in *Sam The Sudden* turns upon the house Mon Repos being a much larger establishment later divided into two semi-detached homes. This, too, had its basis in Wodehouse's own experience. *Sam The Sudden* is set in Valley Fields by which name Dulwich came to be known in Wodehouse's fictional world. When Wodehouse's parents lived in Dulwich they did so at a house in Croxted Road, one of two houses created out of a single residence. Writing a preface for the 1972 edition of *Sam The Sudden*, Wodehouse acknowledges that Valley Fields is Dulwich and hopes 'that in the thirty years since I have seen it Valley Fields has not ceased to be a fragrant backwater. Though I did read somewhere about a firm of builders wanting to put up a block of flats in Croxted Road where I once lived.' This news item had already been recycled into *Company For Henry*:

> 'I met a man who has a house in Croxley Road... he was an old inhabitant and it was his opinion that all these building operations were turning Valley Fields from a peaceful rural retreat into a sort of suburban Manchester. He said he was thankful he was clearing out... he said he would be able to sell his house, because some syndicate or association or whatever you call these concerns wanted to build a block of flats in Croxley Road and his residence came right into the middle of the chunk of land they were planning to do it on.'

If Wodehouse wrote about a setting, he liked to have a particular place in his mind's eye so he would know what it looked like. This applies equally to golf courses as to buildings as all his golfing stories were set at Great Neck golf club, where had been a member. This appears to have been for comfort rather than any practical benefit: could anyone recreate what any of his settings actually looked like, or work out the layout of the rooms in any of the country houses from his descriptions? *Love Among the Chickens* is dedicated to Joan, Effie and Ernestine Bowes-Lyon, grand-daughters of the 12th Earl of Strathmore and Kinghorne and first cousins of Queen Elizabeth the Queen Mother. He would take tea with them at their London house and visited them at their country place at Lyme Regis. This is the setting for the novel. When he came to rewrite it for its 1921 publication he changed the name to Combe Regis. It was an oddity of Wodehouse's that he would change names slightly, while still leaving the genesis obvious to anyone interested.

Hunstanton Hall, where Wodehouse stayed as a guest and also rented himself, is the setting for *Money For Nothing*, and the Octagon there pops up in the grounds of Aunt Agatha's county house. At Hunstanton Hall Wodehouse would write seated in a punt in the moat, with his Monarch typewriter balanced on his knees.

Wodehouse had acquired this typewriter on his first visit to America, and was to rely on it, finding he could not get on with any other. He bought other models to replace it when it seemed beyond all resurrection, but he gave up on them and returned to his faithful Monarch. The company which had made it went out of business, which did not help his efforts to keep it up and running, but it was always patched up somehow, although by the end there was scarcely an original part left. He managed to acquire an identical model, but in time it had to be broken up to provide replacement parts for the original. No-one else was allowed to touch this typewriter, and wherever he went Wodehouse took charge of it on the journey. The typewriter was temperamental: if used too often it would break down, if too infrequently the keys would go stiff, and it required frequent ministrations from the typewriting doctor fraternity. In 1935 it finally expired, beyond all hope of redemption even though, as with those few he loved deeply, he was always ready to lavish money in its direction. It was replaced by a Royal, which in turn was replaced by an electric model in 1956. Electric was a viable option by then for he had settled down to one location; previously his typewriter had travelled with him, and he would write wherever he was - at the golf club, on a punt in a moat, on ocean liners. By 1956 all his writing was being done from his study at home.

Hunstanton was also behind the nomenclature of Lord Hunstanton who appears in *The Small Bachelor*. The names Wodehouse chose for his characters were frequently those of places he knew. The area around Hunstanton was particularly fertile ground in this respect and provided Wodehouse with the lords Heacham, Brancaster and Snettisham and the middle part of J. Sheringham Adair.

Wodehouse lived at Threepwood, which was across the way from Beach Road, Emsworth which gave him three of the names for his Blandings series. Lord Bosham and Lady Ann Warblington also take their names from the locality and Colonel Mant gets his name from the agent who used to oversee Threepwood when he was absent. Emsworth had been renowned for its oysters until a typhoid scare put paid to this local industry. This particular piece of Emsworth's history is given to Belpher, Blandings alter ego.

Wodehouse's first London lodgings were in Markham Square. He disliked them, and in *Ukridge* we are told that Markham Square is 'a dismal backwater' where Ukridge once had rooms. Ukridge has since moved to Arundel Street Leicester Square, where William Townend had digs. Arundell Street (with a double 'l') is where Ashe Marston and Joan Valentine are living at the start of *Something Fresh*. In 1913 Wodehouse stayed with Charles Bovill at an apartment in Prince Of Wales Mansions. This address pops up frequently. In *Summer Lightning* Ronnie Fish takes his intended to the family's London house, 17 Norfolk Street (now Dunraven Street). This was Wodehouse's townhouse. Aunt Dahlia's London house, 47 Charles Street, was the home of Ian Hay, Wodehouse's friend and collaborator on plays.

Wodehouse would know the address well as he once worked by correspondence on a script with Ian Hay when he was in Hollywood.

Collaboration gave Wodehouse the ideas for many plots. Out of the £31. 5s 8d he made from *Love Among The Chickens*, Wodehouse gave Townend £10 for providing the raw material of the plot. *The Luck Stone*, an early trashy boys' adventure story, was written in collaboration with Westbrook. Another magazine serial, *A Man Of Means*, was written in collaboration with Charles Bovill. Most of Wodehouse's theatrical work was written in collaboration.

His theatre work also gave him the plots for many of his novels - and vice versa. Plays were turned into novels and novels into plays. A particularly notable example was *The Old Reliable*. As Edward Everett Horton was looking for a play with a strong butler's role in it, Wodehouse adapted *Spring Fever* for the stage and Horton's American audiences. Horton's commitments prevented him from putting the play on, and, as the play was no longer a straight copy of *Spring Fever*, Wodehouse then set about re-adapting the play into a novel, thereby creating *The Old Reliable*.

Barmy In Wonderland was an adaptation of George S. Kaufman's play *The Butter And Egg Man*. It took him three months to adapt and the pair split the royalties 50-50. It also uses Wodehouse's recent experience of touring with a play where the leading actor was a drunk. *Do Butlers Burgle Banks*? was written from a play of Guy Bolton's, *Money In The Bank*.

The most unsatisfactory novelisation of a play script is *Ring For Jeeves*. This comes from a play Guy Bolton wrote with Wodehouse called *Come On, Jeeves*. The theatrical background of the novel is obvious in the setting and action, but it works well as a story. But not as a Jeeves one, for Jeeves acts out of character. Had the butler part - and Jeeves is a butler in this novel - been given to another character then that would have been fine. As it is, the work detracts from itself as Jeeves ceases to be a credible character in this novel in light of what we know of him elsewhere. Jeeves got into the play as Bolton had written a major part for a butler, and asked his good friend Wodehouse if he could use the name Jeeves for this character, as it would be good for box office. (In fact it never received a West End run out, but it was performed in the provinces.) Wodehouse presumably persevered with Jeeves in this role when he came to write the script up as a novel because a Jeeves story would be good for book sales, too. Wodehouse the businessman had overcome Wodehouse the artist. But Wodehouse was always a businesslike writer. The writers he admired were those who turned out their regular amount of words for a decent income.

Wodehouse could also be ruthless with characters in his novels. Though short-story plots would be based around the characters concerned, with his novels the characters had to do, and be, what the plot demanded, hence such oddities as Monty Bodkin losing his aristocratic background because the plot requires it. Similarly the Empress of Blandings can sometimes be manhandled by a single person whereas at other times she requires a minimum of two to shift her according to the needs of the plot.

The novel *Doctor Sally* is based upon Wodehouse's play *Good Morning, Bill*. This in turn had been based upon a play by the Hungarian Ladislas Fodor. Wodehouse would have worked from a translation of the original play. *The Small Bachelor* is based upon the musical comedy *Oh, Lady! Lady!* the second of the shows which Wodehouse, Bolton and Kern wrote for the Princess Theatre. But the plot has been vastly expanded as the original script ran to only 15,000 words, and so new characters and plot lines were added for the novel. *Doctor Sally* however is a very thin work, reflecting more slavish devotion to the script of the play, just as the novel *If I Were You* is also obviously a neat play in different clothing.

In taking the basis of a plot from another writer to create *Doctor Sally*, Wodehouse was only doing what he had done in the past. The idea for *Uncle Fred Flits By* was developed from a suggestion by William Townend, to whom Wodehouse would write asking if he had any spare plots which he might like to offload on his friend. For his part, Wodehouse would also make plot suggestions to Townend. The pair worked in very different genres and so while the ideas one had might well be unsuitable for their own work it could be relevant for the other. Another from whom Wodehouse would solicit ideas was Bob Davis, the editor of *Munsey's Magazine*. Davis would suggest plots to his writers - Wodehouse admits they were not normally very good - and then buy the resulting story from them. From this process came *The Coming Of Bill*, a very strange Wodehouse product. It is a saga rather than a light novel and there are two deaths in it, including a friend of the hero. It concerns the falling apart of a marriage and the subsequent patching up of the union. Interestingly, this marriage is based on a brief courtship with the bride and groom hardly knowing one another. This is the basis of most of the happy endings in Wodehouse's novels, but here it is suggested that it does not necessarily make for a happy foundation of married life. The force for bad in the book is provided by an aunt who butts in with her strange views on child rearing and also views the father of the child as 'the enemy.' The whole thing is a bit too unbelievable to take seriously as a real slice-of-life drama, but it is definitely closer to that than a light Wodehouse farce. Wodehouse's talents were wasted writing a book like this.

Wodehouse could write about real people and situations - as a great adapter he frequently did - but he needed to clothe them with the Wodehouse treatment. The starkness of *The Coming Of Bill* makes it a strange bedfellow with most of the rest of the Wodehouse oeuvre. Wodehouse claimed that the plot did not matter, only the treatment, but here it shows that the plot does matter. If the plot is not suitable for the Wodehouse treatment, then the treatment cannot work. The failure of this novel illustrates Wodehouse's great success elsewhere with this technique.

Many of Wodehouse's characters are based on people he knew, either from meeting them or reading about them. That Spode leads the black shorts because all the shirts had run out is a masterly piece of satire by Wodehouse. Not only does it make Spode look as daft as the author is keen to make him out to be, but it also reflects the political situation at the time. The British Union of Fascists, whose leader Wodehouse was attacking in particular, wore black shirts, the British Fascist Association wore brown ones, Commander Locker-Hampton's anti-Communists vigilantes were garbed in blue ones, Major Douglas' Social Credit movement wore green shirts and the Independent Labour Party's Guild of Youth took red shirts as their uniform.

Lord Tilbury, formerly Sir George Pyke, is based upon Lord Northcliffe. Tilbury House, the centre of the Pyke empire is given the same location as Northcliffe House. Blumenfield, who relies upon his twelve-year old son for his artistic decisions on the basis that what appeals to a twelve-year old will appeal to the general public, has copied Abraham Erlanger's familial arrangement and methods of working.

It is not only the humans of Wodehouse's acquaintance which made it into his work. When Wodehouse's parents returned to England they bought a dog, a mongrel called Bob, who gets into the supporting cast, under his own name, in *Love Among The Chickens*. Ethel and Plum Wodehouse were also great dog lovers, and one of their pekes, Susan, gets a walk-on part in *The Go Getter*. Norman Murphy, in his fascinating *In Search Of Blandings* has shown that you can have a fair old stab at working out the chronology of Wodehouse's books simply by knowing which dog he owned at the time as there are often references to them. For instance, the Mixer stories are written by a bulldog, which is the type of dog Wodehouse had at the time. The only dog the Wodehouses could not get on with was an Aberdeen terrier, which they gave away. Bertie Wooster could not take to this terrier either when it appeared in the chronicles as Stiffy Byng's Bartholemew.

Ukridge and Lord Uffenham are based upon people Wodehouse knew as, in a different sense, was James Orlebar Cloyster. Psmith was based upon someone he had been told about. Once he had a character, or came across one, he could develop others from it. Psmith is the genesis of many of the characters in Wodehouse novels. Lord Ickenham is an obvious development of the Psmith character, but so too are figures such as Jimmy Crocker and Joe Vanringham, who appear in books published 20 years apart. Bertie Wooster is an evolution of another character Wodehouse wrote about, and this in turn was simply an adaptation of the typical stage dude figure. Sometimes no adaptation was required. Most of Wodehouse's butlers are simply stage butlers. Lord Emsworth, an elderly man prone to absent-mindedness, is not a type of character previously unknown in the world of humorous writing.

With Wodehouse the genius lay in what he did with his raw materials, not the raw materials themselves. He just took what was already readily at hand and fashioned something on which was left his own imprint.

The quest for plots and incidents was a never-ending one. Wodehouse would buy them from others if necessary, or adapt those he came across. Gally was a member of the Pelican Club, whose activities provided Wodehouse with his basis for the Clothes Stakes in *Uncle Fred In The Springtime*, which is a retelling in adapted form of the story of The Great Hat Stakes, organised by Joe Scott, whereby the first hat to come through the door of the American Bar of the Criterion after 7pm would be the winner. Odds were offered on wide range of headgear, with a black top hat at 11-10, a bowler at 6-4 and 9-4 on an opera hat. Just after 7pm a waiter from a nearby restaurant came through the doors. He was an Indian waiter wearing a turban and was almost certainly bribed by Scott to make an entrance at that juncture. Scott leapt to his feet and embraced the Indian declaring 'Twenty-eight and a half quid in the book and not a penny laid on it.' Mustard Pott similarly cleans up with insider information in the Clothes Stakes, when first through the door is someone he has locked in the club's telephone booth and who is still in his outfit from the previous night's fancy dress party.

Sometimes Wodehouse's inspiration is obvious, such as his short story *Mr Potter Takes A Rest Cure* which is his take on Saki's *The Lull*, and his *The Secret Pleasures Of Reginald*, which was published in *Vanity Fair* in 1915, is so written that it could be slipped into a Saki anthology without many people noticing. Reginald is even the name of one of Saki's main characters. There must be many long-forgotten stories in magazines which gave Wodehouse a germ of an idea to which he could give the Wodehouse treatment, but he also took inspiration from his own work. A regular short story plot is the young man behaving out of character to impress a girl he wants to marry, she being unsure if this would be a good match as he seemed too perfect, and some incident causes him to revert to his more typical behaviour, whereupon the girl realises that he was not as she had imagined and that he was her ideal mate after all. This idea even surfaces twice within the same collection of short stories, *A Few Quick Ones* in *The Right Approach* and *Joy Bells For Walter*. At least these appear as the third and eighth stories in the collection. In *The Man With Two Left*, the first story, *Bill The Bloodhound* is about Alice Weston, a chorus girl who is not prepared to marry out of the profession. The second story, *Extricating Young Gussie*, relies upon a father forbidding his daughter's marriage to someone not on the stage.

The same ideas would come round time and time again, as would the same character-types. Wodehouse was aware of this, sending himself up nicely in his introduction to *Summer Lightning*:

A certain critic - for such men, I regret to say, do exist - made the nasty remark about my last novel that it contained 'all the old Wodehouse characters under different names'. He has probably by now been eaten by bears, like the children who made mock of the prophet Elisha: but if he still survives he will not be able to make a similar charge against *Summer Lightning*. With my superior intelligence, I have outgeneralled the man this time by putting in all the old Wodehouse characters under the same names. Pretty silly it will make him feel, I rather fancy.

Once Wodehouse had the idea for a plot of a novel he would write out a detailed structure, often as much as a third of the length of the finished work. Into this he would also set down bits of dialogue in skeleton form to be written up later. It was the forming of the plot that was his main concern: he averred that he always thought that in writing the book he was wasting valuable time, as the difficult part of writing was in drawing up the plot. Beginnings of books often caused him problems and these would frequently be rewritten over and over again. He would have difficulties in organising the action so as to bring all of his major characters in to play a scene and making sure that the plot lines had been introduced evenly throughout the text. In *Performing Flea* he writes about *Uncle Fred In The Springtime*:

> After writing 150 pages I have about 40 which are right. Every time I write a book I swear I'll never write another with a complicated plot. In this one - in the first 40 pages - I have either brought on to play a scene or mentioned heavily each of my principal characters - ten including Lord Emsworth's pig. So the going ought to be easier now.

Wodehouse felt that unless his plots moved slickly they were inclined to bore the reader. Often he would be left with loose ends and incongruities. Frequently one plus one cannot equal two for Wodehouse's plot to work and normally he recognises this and puts in an explanation of why the obvious cannot happen. Sometimes, though, Wodehouse's plots stretch credibility too far. In *Sam The Sudden*, Sam dispossesses a burglar of his trousers to prevent him scarpering while he toddles next door to hob-nob with the neighbours. Why does the burglar, left free to roam around Sam's house, not just go upstairs and help himself to a pair of Sam's trousers? The answer is that the plot needs Lord Tilbury to enter the house and be robbed of his trousers. Normally Wodehouse would have spotted the flaw, and written in some excuse as to why the burglar cannot just pinch a pair of Sam's trousers, but here he forgets. *French Leave*, one of the most disappointing of his novels, leaves a lot of loose ends. What happens to the money Old Nick nicked from Mrs Pegler? What happened to the dossier Quibolle? Why does Old Nick have to escape using the balcony when the police do not know that he is a criminal? Too many characters have too little to do. Jo Trent just drops out halfway through. What was her point, except to have a maid called Fellowes? And, what, really was the need for that? Kate Trent does not really do anything, and she is neither the voice of authority nor does she provide an obstacle to be overcome. The novel is based, loosely, upon a play of Guy Bolton's *Three Blind Mice* about three sisters who run a small farm and set out to blow their inheritance in a quest for husbands and happiness, but somewhere the whole has become a disjointed conjunction of ideas.

Once Wodehouse had sorted the plot out tightly then he was confident with the writing process and could steam ahead. Problems occurred when, as he termed it, the plot 'went off the rails' as he was writing it. When it was clear in his mind, and transferred neatly to the paper, the writing process would be very rapid. The final 40,000 words of *Leave It To Psmith* - in other words about the second half of the book - took him three weeks to write. Once he had got a completed story written he felt he had broken the back of the work, and could concentrate on the bit he particularly relished, the tinkering and polishing. As he got older this process took longer and played a greater part in the whole operation. In an interview in 1971 for *The Guardian* he told Richard Usborne:

> I'm always re-reading and re-writing what I've written. You put it down straight first time. Then you fiddle with it, change it, change it again, and it gets better.

Frequently this revision process could also involve the changing of plots as ideas might be added or taken away, as could characters. The serial *Uncle Fred In The Springtime*, written for the *Saturday Evening Post*, is a case in point, as the magazine decided that the plot was too complicated to be followed on a weekly basis, and so Wodehouse dropped one plot line and a couple of characters. The novel as published in book form was the original, longer version. Magazine stories and serials could also be rewritten before being published in book form. Sometimes this could amount to minor tinkerings, at other times substantial rewrites, such as when he formed the novel *Laughing Gas* from a 16,000-word, four-part magazine series. Public complaints about the ending of *Leave It To Psmith* when it was serialised lead to Wodehouse writing a new ending for book publication. Novels would also get transformed into magazine series. *The Swoop*, which was only published in Britain, was rewritten in 1916 for *Vanity Fair* about an invasion of America.

American editions of his works were often slightly different from English ones, and occasionally there were major changes. *Something New* (the American title for *Something Fresh*) included a 20-page scene which was taken from *Mike*, which had not been published in America. When Wodehouse submitted *The Luck of the Bodkins* to the *Saturday Evening Post*, the magazine rejected it. In a much shortened - by about a quarter - version it was accepted by the *Red Book* in America and *The Passing Show* in Britain. The American book publication used the text of the magazine version, while his British publishers preferred the fuller, original version.

The Prince And Betty was originally written for an American audience, and received magazine serialisation in May 1912. The story was a straightforward romance. For book publication in America, Wodehouse interweaved the plot from *Psmith, Journalist*, which had been serialised in Britain but not America. However, in England A & C Black were to publish *Psmith, Journalist*, and so the British version of *The Prince And Betty* was published in its original form as a straightforward romance story, by Mills & Boon. As a further indication of how Wodehouse would reuse material, the American version of *The Prince And Betty* was rewritten as a five-part serial, *A Prince For Hire*, which appeared in the American *Illustrated Love Magazine* in 1931.

My Man Jeeves includes the only four stories about Reggie Pepper which made it into book publication (and then only in Britain). Reggie Pepper is the catalyst for Bertie Wooster. Wodehouse, the great adapter, fashioned the character of Reggie Pepper from that of the standard stage dude, and then modified this figure to create Bertie Wooster. But Wooster was not born as a fully formed character. The early Bertie Wooster still has strong traces of a stage dude about him, with the stories punctuated with lots of 'don't you knows', just as the Pepper stories are. As Wooster evolved into a more rounded character over the course of these early stories, so too did Jeeves. Jeeves' tastes also became more upmarket. In the magazine version of the sole short story narrated by Jeeves he calls Bertie 'the guv'nor'. Wodehouse changed this for the book publication of this story to reflect a more educated Jeeves. The early Jeeves of *My Man Jeeves* is not the well-read Jeeves of later works.

The four Jeeves stories in *My Man Jeeves* were to reappear in *Carry On, Jeeves*. The plots of three of the Reggie Pepper stories were also to reappear. *Doing Clarence A Bit Of Good* becomes *Jeeves Makes An Omelette*, while *Helping Freddie* is reproduced virtually word for word as the Jeeves story *Fixing it For Freddie*, with Jeeves taking on the role played by one of Pepper's friends. *Rallying Round Old George* later becomes a Mulliner story, *George And Alfred*. Only seven Pepper stories were published in magazines.

Reggie Pepper first appeared in September 1911 in *Helping Freddie* in *The Strand*. He is a young man about town, who lives off the wealth inherited from his uncle who was a colliery owner. He narrates his own tales and describes himself as 'a chap who's supposed to be one of the biggest chumps in London'. [*Disentangling Old Percy*] Pepper is a more self-centred character than Bertie. Bertie's head is full of ideas of performing valiant deeds for his friends, and he has a strict code of honour. It is this which causes him problems. Reggie Pepper is less virtuous, and so has less of a chance to get into scrapes. Pepper is a more earthy character than Wooster:

> 'Have you ever heard of Eunice Nugent?'
> 'Not to my knowledge.'
> 'As she doesn't sprint up and down the joy-way at the Hippodrome, I don't suppose you would.'
> I thought this rather uncalled for, seeing that, as a matter of fact, I scarcely know a dozen of the Hippodrome chorus. [*Concealed Art*]
> 'The Booles have asked me down to their place for the week-end, and I don't know whether to go or not. You see, they have family prayers at half-past eight sharp, and besides that there's a frightful risk of music after dinner. On the other hand, young Roderick Boole thinks he can play piquet.'
> 'I should go,' I said. [*Disentangling Old Percy*]

Disentangling Old Percy, which did not make book publication, is the best of the Pepper stories. It is well plotted, with plenty of twists, and well written:

'I hardly expected so sensible a suggestion from you, Reginald,' she said. 'It is a very good plan. It shows that you really have a definite substratum of intelligence; and it is all the more deplorable that you should idle your way through the world as you do, when you might be performing some really useful work.'

That was Florence all over. Even when she patted you on the head she did it with her knuckles.

The Florence in the story is Florence Craye, who with her brother Edwin was to appear in the Wooster chronicles. However by Wooster time her brother had become a boy scout; here he is her elder brother and is called Lord Weeting.

Reggie Pepper gets into fixes which he has to labour out of himself. He has no Jeeves to turn to, though his manservant appears in *Rallying Round Old George* and, whilst promising fidelity, double-crosses his master. *The Good Angel* features a butler, Keggs, who gets involved in manipulating the love lives of the guests for his own ends to ensure he wins the servants' sweepstake as to whom the daughter of the house will marry. To this end Keggs rows out to an island to untie a boat so as to maroon a couple there, and offers advice on courtship to the guest whose name he has drawn. Wodehouse the great recycler returns to this idea in *A Damsel In Distress*, in which one of the sub-plots concerns Keggs the butler's machinations to win the sweepstake, which involves blackmail and double-crossing. Whereas in *The Good Angel* the advice he offered was genuine, in the novel he offers deliberately misleading advice to Lord Percy, the eldest son of his employer, apparently in support of Lord Percy's aims, but in fact to further his own interests only. *The Good Angel* - which was published in America as *Matrimonial Sweepstakes* - was collected into *The Man Upstairs*. Another story in this collection, *By Advice Of Counsel*, is about Gentleman Bailey double crossing a friend with advice on how to get married with the intention of keeping him single so as to maintain Gentleman Bailey's way of life, which is supported by his bachelor friend.

Through these characters and situations Wodehouse was gathering together the ideas and characters which were to lead towards his greatest literary creation, the relationship between Jeeves and Wooster.

Jeeves

Jeeves is the most famous butler in the world, his fame so great that not even the fact that he is not a butler has been able to diminish it.

He is a gentleman's gentleman, a valet, an employer's personal attendant. The men of the families who lived in the grand houses when Wodehouse began his writing career would have been expected to have valets to look after their clothes. They might also have had their meals at table served by them, although this may have been done by butler and footmen, depending on the house's particular arrangements.

The role of gentleman's gentlemen is a product of the Edwardian period. They served a need which arose, and later disappeared, as a result of social change. Prior to marriage, the sons of the upper classes lived at home where all their domestic requirements were catered for. All they needed to do was turn up for events in the correct - and properly maintained - garb. For this they employed their own valet. When they left home to get married they would then establish their own domestic staff to run their household.

But when social fashions changed and, instead of remaining at the family home, bachelor sons of upper-class families started to move away, they needed someone to look after their domestic requirements. The choice was to move into rooms, where there would be someone to look after their needs, such as the situation Ukridge is in with Bowles, a former butler - though a more famous relationship of this kind in fiction is

Sherlock Holmes' with Mrs Hudson - or to take a flat, and employ a gentleman's gentleman to look after them.

A gentleman's gentleman is the personal servant of a gentleman, and usually his sole one. He would be responsible for his employer's general welfare, combining the duties of a valet with that of cooking his employer's meals.

The nature of the relationship between an employer and his gentleman depended upon the personalities concerned, both in terms of duties and their personal interaction. The Edwardian era saw a loosening of formality, with children growing to adulthood rebelling against the rigid codes of their parents' generation, a process accentuated by the Great War, where all social classes stood, and fell, side by side in the trenches.

Bertie is very much part of this new generation, impatient with stuffy convention and constantly challenging it in respect to his clothing. He horrifies the older generation, as represented by his Aunt Agatha, by discussing his affairs in front of Jeeves, and his attitude towards Jeeves is generally a pally, confiding one. In return, Jeeves, presumably of the older generation, is guarded - and extremely formal - in his language, and will sometimes remark when asked to offer an opinion or do something that it is 'hardly my place, sir.' Bertie criticises Jeeves for not being 'in tune with modern progressive thought, his attitude being described, perhaps, as hidebound' [*Stiff Upper Lip, Jeeves*], and his battles with him over choice of clothes is not just one of taste, it is one of the generation gap.

'Oh Jeeves,' I said, 'about that check suit.'
'Yes, sir?'
'Is it really a frost?'
'A trifle too bizarre, sir, in my opinion.'
'But lots of fellows have asked me who my tailor is.'
'Doubtless in order to avoid him, sir.'
'He's supposed to be one of the best men in London.'

'I am saying nothing against his moral character, sir.'
[*Jeeves Takes Charge*]

That a gentleman's gentleman and his master lived in close confinement would also bring down barriers. Jeeves' quarters one would expect to consist of the kitchen - where he can entertain his guests - and a bedroom, which is likely to be directly off the kitchen. When Jeeves types, Bertie can hear it; when Bertie needs Jeeves he does not summon him by bell from the far reaches of a voluminous house, closeted away behind a green baize door, he merely calls out for him.

A butler is usually the head of the household staff, which could number dozens of people, and is in charge of wines and the dining table as well as running the household staff, probably with the help of the housekeeper. Bachelor Bertie has no need of a butler. When he entertains guests to meals in his flat, Jeeves will butle for him, just as he does when Bertie eats alone at home. However, were Bertie to get married and set up his own household, then someone of his position and wealth would employ a butler with a household staff under him. He would no longer have the need for a gentleman's gentleman. This is something Jeeves is acutely aware of:

I had no desire to sever a connection so pleasant in every respect as his and mine had been, and my experience is that when the wife comes in at the front door the valet of bachelor days goes out at the back.
[*Bertie Changes His Mind*]

When Bertie is in danger of getting married, he can rely upon Jeeves to conspire to prevent it. As Bertie almost invariably wants out of the engagement himself, this leads him to believe that Jeeves is faithfully rallying round his young master, when Jeeves is merely acting self-interestedly. But Jeeves is prepared to break off an engagement of Bertie's whether Bertie wants it or not - and does in the case of his engagement to Florence Craye in *Jeeves Takes Charge*.

The richness of the humour from the Wooster/Jeeves chronicles arises from the difference between perception and reality. The most obvious is the way that servant conspires against master, while master complacently congratulates himself on having someone who serves him so faithfully and selflessly.

Jeeves is highly selfish, always alert to how he can turn any situation to his own advantage. Asked to smooth a way for Bingo Little to gain an uncle's consent to marry a waitress, Jeeves manipulates the situation so that Bingo's uncle gets engaged to his own cook, who is Jeeves' fiancée. Jeeves has tired of her and wants instead to move in on Bingo Little's intended. When, in *The Metropolitan Touch*, Bingo Little's latest love affair goes wrong, Jeeves, who has been advising Bingo, makes sure that he is in a position to benefit from it by buying the book that was being run on the outcome. The short stories often end with Jeeves financially enhanced. In *Clustering Round Young Bingo* Jeeves so successfully plays the parties off each other that he ends up being rewarded by all involved: £20 from Bingo Little, £25 from Aunt Dahlia, £25 from Uncle Tom Travers, £10 from Uncle George, and even £5 from Bertie even though he says, 'I don't know why I'm giving it to you.'

When asked by Lord Worplesdon how he might arrange to meet J. Chichester Clam in secret, he suggests Bertie take a cottage at Steeple Bumpleigh - where Bertie is dead set against going because it is the lair of his Aunt Agatha - purely because he wants to go fishing there. Jeeves contrives to take whatever holidays or trips he fancies, be it a jaunt to Monte Carlo to play the tables or a round-the-world cruise, under the guise of working for Bertie - and thus at Bertie's expense - and normally in opposition to Bertie's wishes.

Nor does Jeeves treat Bertie with much respect. Outwardly yes, but in subtle ways no:

'I think it would be best for me to stop at Mr Fittleworth's residence, appraise him of what has occurred, deposit the luggage and warn him of your coming.'
'Is warn the word?'
'"Inform" I should have said sir.' [*Joy In The Morning*]

Or more subtly:

'I give you fair warning that, if he tells me I have a face like a fish I shall clump his head.'
'Bertie,' cried the Wickham, contorted with anguish and apprehension and whatnot.
'Yes, I shall.'
'Then you'll simply ruin the whole thing.'
'I don't care. We Woosters have our pride.'
'Perhaps the young gentleman will not notice that you have a face like a fish, sir,' suggested Jeeves. [*The Episode Of The Dog McIntosh*]

Jeeves is indifferent as to whether Bertie suffers or not. Indeed, he can take positive pleasure from seeing Bertie squirm. It is perhaps no coincidence that many of Jeeves' schemes require Bertie to suffer privations. Jeeves arranges for Bertie to go through the humiliating experience of speaking to a girls' school as part of his master plan to preserve the cosy bachelor existence he requires, and writes of it that: 'It was an experience which I should have been sorry to have missed. Mr Wooster, I may say at once, indubitably excelled himself.'

This appears in the short story, *Bertie Changes His Mind*, which is the only one in the canon written by Jeeves. Incidentally, it contains a fine example of humour in Wodehouse's writing which has eluded the anthologists and quotation-compiling merchants, when Jeeves describes the schoolgirls singing their song of welcome to Bertie, prior to him giving his speech:

Considerable latitude of choice was given to the singers in the matter of key, and there was little of what I might call co-operative effort. Each child went on till she reached the end, then stopped and waited for the stragglers to come up. It was an unusual performance, and I, personally, found it extremely exhilarating. It seemed to strike Mr Wooster, however, like a blow. He recoiled a couple of steps and flung up an arm defensively.

Jeeves' schemes to 'solve' Bertie's problems - which often are not Bertie's at all, but those of others which he gets dragged into - often incur physical or mental discomfort to Bertie, frequently gratuitously. He is happy to make his employer writhe:

'And if I am to stave off the Cheesewright challenge, I shall have the need of a weapon. His strength is the strength of ten, and unarmed I shall be corn before his sickle.'
'Extremely well put, sir, if I may say so, and your diagnosis of the situation is perfectly accurate. Mr Cheesewright's robustness would enable him to crush you like a fly.'
'Exactly.'
'He would obliterate you with a single blow. He would break you in two with his bare hands. He would tear you limb from limb.'
I frowned slightly. I was glad to see that he appreciated the gravity of the situation, but these crude physical details seemed to me uncalled for. [*Jeeves And The Feudal Spirit*]

One of Jeeves' stock techniques is to make out that Bertie is insane. This was his solution to the problem of Bertie being credited with the authorship of Rosie M. Banks' novels by

Bingo Little. This was not Bertie's problem but Bingo Little's, and initially developed out of Jeeves' suggestion as to how Bingo might convince his uncle of his intended's suitability as a wife. That Bertie be depicted as a loony was also Jeeves' solution to the problem which Aunt Dahlia and Sir Roderick Glossop face in *Jeeves In The Offing*. In *Stiff Upper Lip, Jeeves*, Jeeves gets Bertie out of his engagement to Madeline Basset by telling her that Bertie is a kleptomaniac producing, as evidence for his claim, the amber statuette that he was supposed to be returning to Pop Basset's collection, announcing that he had found it in Bertie's room. Bertie spends a night in the cells as a result. In this novel Jeeves also telephones Major Plank to come to Totleigh Towers to get Stinker Pinker's address, which Jeeves could quite easily have given him over the telephone. Bertie is endangered by Plank's arrival and has to dive behind a sofa, as Plank thinks that Bertie is a notorious crook. His source for this particular piece of misinformation had been Jeeves in the first place.

At the end of *Right Ho, Jeeves*, Jeeves sends Bertie on an 18-mile bicycle ride to retrieve the key to the back door of Brinkley Court after the house party is locked out, having exited the house summoned by the fire bell rung by Bertie at Jeeves' suggestion. Jeeves has the key all along and lets the party back in after Bertie has left. The suffering of Bertie so cheers up the rest of the house party that animosities between them are quickly forgotten. Had Jeeves wished, there would have been no need for Bertie to make the whole 18-mile journey; Bertie could merely have bicycled around the corner, had a quiet smoke or whatever, and sneaked back into the house later. It would have had the same effect - for all bar Bertie, who, yet again, suffers at Jeeves' hands.

Even when Jeeves does act to save, rather than endanger or embarrass, his employer, he can do so in a rather half-hearted way. When Jeeves intervenes during a scam being carried out on Bertie by Alice Hemmingway and Soapy Sam by deftly lifting a pearl case from Soapy Sam's pocket when he helps him on with his coat, Bertie is all grateful thanks, and gives him £20 by way of appreciation. Yet Jeeves had recognised the man as a conman, from an earlier occurrence, but stood passively by, watching, while Bertie was relieved of £100. In this instance Jeeves has nothing to gain bar the pleasure of seeing his employer lose £100.

Another occasion where Jeeves strictly regulates the dispersal of his help occurs in the story *The Episode Of The Dog McIntosh*. The plot involves substituting a new Aberdeen terrier for Aunt Agatha's one which, while being looked after by Bertie, had given by Roberta Wickham to the Blumenfield kid to suck up to his family for her own purposes. Bertie goes to retrieve the dog from the Blumenfields' hotel suite, while the occupants are at the cinema. Roberta Wickham has a meeting with them afterwards, and is to be shown into their suite when she arrives. Pop Blumenfield, finding himself short of a dog and told by Roberta Wickham, on Jeeves' suggestion, that Bertie is to blame, goes round to confront Bertie, whereupon Jeeves returns the dog, which is in fact another Aberdeen terrier, bought for the purpose. Why did Jeeves not send Bertie out with the replacement dog in the first place? Because by arranging the action as he did, Jeeves gets the chance to insult, very subtly, Pop Blumenfield to his face, humiliate Bertie, who is cowering behind the sofa and enrich himself - Pop Blumenfield gives him £5 in thanks and Bertie gives Jeeves a further £15 in his relief that the ordeal, created by Roberta Wickham and stage-managed by Jeeves, is over.

Not only is Jeeves happy to see Bertie suffer, he will also double-cross him. Asked to hold on to Uncle Willoughby's manuscript of his memoirs prior to destroying them so as to prevent them from being published, Jeeves posts the manuscript to the publishers to break an engagement Bertie is in favour of but he is not. In *Right Ho, Jeeves* Bertie gets Jeeves to agree not to demand the disposal of his mess jacket as his price for helping out. Jeeves agrees to this, but 'accidentally' burns it when ironing.

Jeeves comes across in Bertie's memoirs, despite the overwhelming niceness of its writer, as rather an unpleasant fellow. The characters of the two protagonists are vastly different. Jeeves is immoral, while Bertie has a very strict code. Bertie's code is so strict that it constantly cramps his room for manoeuvre. It requires that he is chivalrous to females to the point where he is unable to break an engagement to a woman, however much he might dislike her. His code also requires that he always helps a pal in distress, and he prides himself on never letting down a friend in need. Jeeves, on the other hand, has no such scruples. He is prepared to steal, lie, bribe, double-cross, blackmail, break promises, and knock policemen unconscious with coshes if the need arises. Bertie is prepared to live a life of hell married to a girl he cannot stand rather than break his code. When Jeeves finds himself engaged to a girl he has grown tired of, he plots to offload her onto another.

Bertie likes to flatter himself, regarding his various battles with Jeeves, that: 'I suppose when two men of iron will live in close association with one another, there are bound to be occasional clashes.' [*The Code Of The Woosters*]. The joke, of course, is that Bertie is weak and allows others to bulldoze their wishes upon him. But Bertie does display great strength of character in living up to his beliefs despite the peril in which they constantly place him. He is aware that his values, so deep-rooted as they are, are often self-defeating:

> I drew no comfort from the fact that Stiffy Byng thought me like Sydney Carton. I had never met the chap, but I gathered that he was somebody who had taken it on the chin to oblige a girl, and to my mind that was enough to stamp him as a priceless ass. Sydney Carton and Bertie Wooster, I felt - nothing to choose between them. Sydney, one of the mugs - Bertram, the same. [*The Code Of The Woosters*]

Part of the humour is that Bertie is sometimes aware of what happens to him, but his overwhelming generosity of spirit blanks it out. He talks of 'the hideous revelation of Jeeves treachery' [*Jeeves And The Yule-Tide Spirit*] but consistently allows his fate to rest in Jeeves' hands. He talks bitterly of aunts, in which he quite clearly includes his Aunt Dahlia, but he always comes running when she calls, and declares that: 'There are few males or females whose society I enjoy more than that of this genial sister of my late father.' [*Much Obliged, Jeeves*] Yet right at the end of the final Wooster novel, Wooster tells Jeeves:

> We are tranquil. And I'll tell you why. There are no aunts here. And in particular we are three thousand miles away from Mrs Dahlia Travers of Brinkley Manor, Market Snodsbury, Worcestershire. Don't get me wrong Jeeves, I like the old flesh and blood. In fact I revere her. Nobody can say she isn't good company. But her moral code is lax. She cannot distinguish between what is according to Hoyle and what is not according to Hoyle. If she wants to do anything, she doesn't ask herself 'would Emily Post approve of this?', she goes on and does it.

Yet, despite being capable of this very shrewd assessment of Dahlia, he continually refers to her as his 'good and deserving aunt', as opposed to Agatha, who gets damned in the strongest terms, with Bertie suggesting that she is a werewolf who eats her young. Yet what does Aunt Agatha ever do to Bertie? All she wants is for him to make a good marriage, get a respectable job and take his family responsibilities with the seriousness that she takes them. Whereas at Dahlia's hands Bertie suffers all forms of degradation and anxiety, and she requires him to do things which risk his going to jail. Indeed, one of his sojourns with Dahlia ends with him spending a night in the cells. Bertie is determined to take the rap for something he had not done, and go to jail rather than allow his aunt to give up her cook, Anatole, which is the price of Bertie's freedom. Dahlia is fundamentally immoral and, unlike Agatha, has great respect for Jeeves, and is fan of his methods. One of these is blackmail, of which Dahlia declares: 'Good old blackmail! You can't beat it. I've always said so and I always shall!' [*The Code Of The Woosters*] Whereas Agatha might be sniffily condescending towards Bertie, she never reaches the height of invective which Dahlia will hurl at her nephew:

> To look at you, one would think you are just an ordinary sort of idiot - certifiable, perhaps, but quite harmless. Yet, in reality, you are a worse scourge than the Black Death. I tell you, Bertie, when I contemplate you I seem to come up against all the underlying sorrow and horror of life with such a thud that I feel as if I had walked into a lamp post. [*Right Ho, Jeeves*]

But Aunt Dahlia is a pal, and Bertie always supports his pals, and excuses them their trespasses on his good nature. Jeeves is another pal, and Bertie is always benevolent towards him in his deeds. He often voluntarily gives up a valued item of clothing as a kindness to Jeeves. Bertie is also generous to him in word: 'I rely on him in every crisis and he never lets me down' [*Jeeves And The Hard Boiled Egg*] and, even more generously:

> There's one thing you have to give Jeeves credit for. He lets the dead past bury its d. He and the young master may have had their differences about Alpine hats with pink feathers in them, but when he see the y. m. on the receiving end of the slings and arrows of outrageous fortune, he sinks his dudgeon and comes through with the feudal spirit at his best. [*Stiff Upper Lip, Jeeves*]

The point being, of course, that Jeeves does not always come to Bertie's aid. Sometimes he pretends to, but acts on his own agenda instead; at other times - when he has the hump with Bertie, such as over his purple socks - he declines to. Bertie, albeit only rather vaguely, is aware of this, but he blots it from his mind. He is not a great rationaliser or analyst. He prefers to presume that everyone is like him, ever eager and conscientious in aiding pals overcome their problems. Unfortunately his pals are not so conscientious. Bertie is perhaps unfortunate in his choice of friends, for he is let down regularly by them. As Lord Chuffnell remarks, 'I wish I had a quid for every time I've seen him take the blame for somebody else's dirty work on his own shoulders.' [*Thank You, Jeeves*] Ma Cream thinks him a half-wit because she discovers him in her son's room searching for a cow-creamer in another's cause. She finds him thus because Roberta Wickham, who was supposed to be keeping guard, abandoned her post to go to the telephone and forgot then all about him. Lord Bittlesham thinks Bertie a loony because he believes Bertie was claiming authorship of Rosie M. Banks' novels, when in fact this claim was foisted on him by Bingo Little.

There is a strong case for saying that Bertie's perceived stupidity is in part a generosity of spirit and a strict adherence to his code. Bertie is a prisoner of his own character and beliefs as much as his intelligence. Quite how stupid is Bertie? Not nearly as much as he is painted, that is for sure. Much of the propaganda concerning Bertie's stupidity comes from Jeeves, who is constantly dropping him in it, by having to rectify situations by a public declaration that Bertie is a loony. When Bertie complains to Jeeves about this, Jeeves dismisses his complaint complacently with 'only to your immediate circle now resident at Brinkley Court, sir.' Bertie retorts that 'You keep saying that, and you must know it is the purest apple sauce. You don't really think the Creams will maintain a tactful reserve? They'll dine out on it for years. Returning to America they'll spread the story from the rock-bound coasts of Maine to the Everglades of Florida.' [*Jeeves In The Offing*]

Bertie's main advocate for his imbecility is himself. He is always telling us that either he or other people believe him to be an ass, though he does let slip that his mother thought him intelligent. We also know that he went to Oxford University, albeit at a time when money as much as intelligence was a requirement of entry, and that he enjoys doing crosswords. Bertie is not scholarly, but then scholarship is not the same as intelligence. Bertie is always puffing Jeeves' intelligence, but how much of what Bertie describes thus is in fact better viewed as cunning and learning? Jeeves is always keen to display the products of his reading - and he is certainly widely read - but someone of Bertie's class and upbringing is unlikely to show off his cleverness; it is not the done thing. It is rather a British trait, especially amongst the upper classes, to downplay one's abilities, and most certainly one's intellectual talents. Sometimes, when Bertie is at pains to make himself look stupid, he clearly is not because he is in on the joke:

> I remember something Jeeves had once called Gussie.
> 'A sensitive plant, what?'
> 'Exactly. You know your Shelley, Bertie.'
> 'Oh, am I?' [*The Code Of The Woosters*]

Or when Bertie is telling Jeeves a story and he wishes the protagonists to be anonymous. Jeeves has suggested calling them A and B, overruling Bertie's suggestion to call them North and South. A third person enters the story and needs a name:

> 'Shall we call him C, sir?
> 'Caesar is as good a name as any, I suppose.' [*Jeeves And The Greasy Bird*]

All in all, Bertie need not be taken as a totally reliable witness where matters of his own intelligence are concerned. He cottons on to the implications of Gussie losing his notebook, when Gussie does not and he realises the jeopardy the syndicate is in from Steggles' discovery that Harold the choirboy can sprint quickly, which had passed Bingo by.

We are led to view Jeeves as a genius because Bertie keeps telling us to. In the first story in *My Man Jeeves*, *Leave It To Jeeves*, Bertie introduces Jeeves as his capable confidant, without whom he would not know what to do. Previously, in the story *Extricating Gussie* in *The Man With Two Left Feet*, Jeeves had been a valet of no significance whatsoever. When Bertie runs into troubles in this story he does not look towards Jeeves for advice, but towards an aunt.

The problem Jeeves is asked to solve in *Leave It To Jeeves* is that of an artist friend of Bertie's, Corky, who has two ambitions: to marry his fiancée and to become a portrait painter. The snags are that he is dependent upon his uncle for a quarterly allowance and no-one has yet commissioned him to paint a portrait. Jeeves takes the case in hand and, as a result, Corky's fiancée ends up married to the uncle instead, and she presents him with an heir, which cuts Corky out of his inheritance. Given his first portrait commission, to paint this child's picture, Corky produces the painting, but his uncle takes exception to it and cuts off Corky's allowance. Jeeves rescues something from the embers by suggesting that Corky use the painting as a basis of a comic series 'The Adventures of Baby Blobbs.' When the series takes off, Corky generously - in view of the fact that he views Jeeves as a 'fool' for his previous scheme that backfired so - rewards Jeeves. But Corky ends up further away from his ambitions than before Jeeves came to his 'help'.

In another of the stories in *My Man Jeeves*, *Jeeves And The Hard Boiled Egg*, Jeeves comes to the aid of Bicky and ends up losing him his allowance. He rescues the situation by suggesting to Bicky a blackmail scheme.

In *Jeeves And The Old School Chum*, Jeeves conspires to break up Mrs Bingo Little's friendship with her old school friend, a food faddist, by depriving the party of its picnic lunch, thus turning Mrs Little against the other's belief in a minimal food intake. Mrs Little is not bothered by missing lunch, and Bertie points out to Jeeves that it is men who object to missing lunch, not women, whose important meal is tea. So Jeeves arranges that the car will run out of petrol in the middle of nowhere when they are returning for tea. This does the trick.

Like Wodehouse, in relation to his skills as a banker, Wooster was self-deprecating:

> Every year, starting about the middle of November, there is a good deal of anxiety and apprehension among owners of the better-class of country-house throughout England as to who will get Bertram Wooster's patronage for the Christmas holidays. It may be one it may be another. As my Aunt Dahlia says, you never know where the blow will fall.
> This year, however, I had decided early. It couldn't have been later than Nov. 10 when a sigh of relief went up from a dozen stately homes as it became known that the short straw had been drawn by Sir Reginald Witherspoon, Bart, of Bleaching Court, Upper Bleaching, Hants. [*The Ordeal Of Young Tuppy*]

Like Wodehouse, Wooster is related to the aristocracy. Indeed, Bertie could well become a leading member of it. The head of the Wooster family is the Earl of Yaxley, formerly Sir George Wooster Bart, Bertie's Uncle George. As this uncle is childless, the earldom will be inherited by a nephew. Which one? The contenders appear to be Bertie and his first cousins Claude and Eustace. The question is: which of George's brothers is the elder? Bertie's father, or his Uncle Henry, Claude and Eustace's begetter? No clues are offered. Bertie does not talk of his father, and Henry is noted only for doing 'some rummy things' amongst them 'keeping eleven pet rabbits in his bedroom. In fact he wound up his career, happy to the last and completely surrounded by rabbits in some sort of home.' [*The Inimitable Jeeves*] The second Earl of Kimberley became a recluse after the death of his wife. When necessity forced a visit to a London doctor, he arrived at the train station just too late to catch his train, threw a turnip at the station clock and broke it, and stomped off back to Kimberley, where he would allow no visits. After his death, his executors came from London and found living at Kimberley in harmony together a string of mistresses and their offspring.

Bertie writes of his white mess jacket that: 'I jolly well intend to fight for it with all the vim of grand old Sieur de Wooster at the Battle of Agincourt.' [*Right Ho, Jeeves*] A Wodehouse ancestor fought at the Battle of Agincourt. Sir John Wodehouse, a Wodehouse 16 generations before Plum, was a Commissioner of Array for Norfolk charged with raising troops for French campaign, and an executor to Henry V's will. His descendants took 'Agincourt' as their motto. Bertram is a name which appears on the Wodehouse family tree. Sir Bertram de Wodehouse married the daughter of Hamo, Lord of Felton and distinguished himself fighting for Edward I against the Scots in the 13th century. Bertie defends his decision to keep playing the banjo with: 'A fellow simply can't go on truckling - do I mean truckling? I know it begins with a t - to his valet for ever. There comes a time when he must remember that his ancestors did dashed well at the Battle of Crecy and put the old foot down.' [*Thank You, Jeeves*]

Wooster and Wodehouse have more in common in the matter of names, which extended to Christian names they preferred to suppress, in Bertie's case his second:

'I didn't know your name was Wilberforce.'

I explained that except in moments of great emotion one hushed it up. [*The Mating Season*]

Bertie gained the name Wilberforce because his father won a packet on an outsider of that name in the Grand National the day before his christening. Over money the author and his creation share similarities. Both were wealthy men - at least by the time the Wooster novels were being written - and so untroubled by worries of how to pay the next bill, but neither was reckless with their money. Bertie turns down the chance to invest £1,000 in a play and could be keenly aware of small sums:

> The going was sticky and took about eight and elevenpence off the value of my Sure-grip tennis shoes in the first two yards. [*Jeeves And The Impending Doom*]
>
> A man who has just become engaged to a girl whose whole personality gives him a sinking feeling and who has had to pay thirty-five quid to a blood-sucker and another twopence to a lending library for a dud book is seldom in mid-season form. [*Aunts Aren't Gentlemen*]

Bertie could be generous to his friends with his largesse. So, too, could Wodehouse when dealing with his own family and close friends; in particular William Townend, a prolific, but worst-selling author. Wodehouse supported Townend financially for many years, and ran a separate bank account for him to enable this married man to continue writing. Wodehouse also used his connections and reputation to try to boost his friend's prospects. This was down to friendship, not from a belief in Townend's books which, as he confessed after Townend's death, he found dull.

In playing the banjo, the two Ws share a short-lived hobby. Wodehouse was learning the instrument as a young man until, so the story goes, Westbrook pawned it and then lost the ticket. Longer lived activities that they shared were a love for golf and music theatre. Bertie had a cousin who was a theosophist; Plum's brother was head of the Theosophical College in Benares. Both went to a prep school called Malvern House. Bertie tried to marry into musical comedy; his ghostwriter succeeded at it. Both hated public speaking and were no good at it. At the dinner after the ceremony granting his honorary doctorate from Oxford, Wodehouse was called upon, by the hall shouting 'we want Wodehouse!', to say a few words after the formal speeches. A few words were all his audience got. The microphone was passed down the table to him, he stood and mumbled into it 'thank you,' and sat down.

It is unavoidable that a writer writing in the first person will end up putting something of themselves into the 'I' character. But Wodehouse put a considerable deal of himself into Bertie Wooster, and on one occasion Bertie seems to be talking more of Wodehouse than himself:

'The whole trouble is due to your blasted aunt.'
'Which blasted aunt? Specify, old thing. I have so many.' [*Clustering Round Young Bingo*]

Bertie only reveals four aunts of his own in his chronicles. Wodehouse had five times this number. When Bertie writes that: 'I don't wonder that all these author blokes have bald heads' [*Clustering Round Young Bingo*] it is Wodehouse he is describing.

Like Wooster, Wodehouse was not a witty man. His conversation did not sparkle over the dinner table with bon mots. Bertie Wooster is one of the funniest writers in the English language, yet he seldom cracks a joke. One of the extremely rare witticisms he ventures occurs when, asked how he was after a night in the cells, he replies 'I have a pinched look' [*Jeeves And the Feudal Spirit*]. Bertie's memoirs may be considered humorous because of many factors - the juxtaposition of images, the mangling of phrases and similes, the undercurrents of tension between the various protagonists, the deceits and conceits, the cock-eyed view of the world - but never because Bertie has set out to write an overtly funny piece.

Those who met Wodehouse hoping to be dazzled by witticisms or badinage were disappointed. What they encountered instead was a well-mannered, polite upper-class gentleman who was as happy, and normally happier, listening than talking. As Duff Copper remembers: 'I sat next to a man I thought was charming [and] because he was humble I was patronising. When I left, I casually asked the head waiter who the gentleman was I had been sitting next to. 'Mr PG Wodehouse.' I wish I had been nicer. [*A Durable Fire: The Letters of Duff and Diana Cooper 1890-1954*] Frank Crowninshield wrote of PG Wodehouse:

> Judged by exterior appearances only, he seemed merely a stodgy and colourless Englishman; silent, careful with his money, self-effacing, slow-witted and matter-of-fact... In all those years - at dinners, at his cottage in the country, on the golf-links, at the Coffee House Club, over a weekend, at the theatre - I never heard him utter a clever, let alone brilliant, remark. No alienist could possibly have guessed him to be the fanciful, erudite and highly intellectual man he actually was.

Bertie Wooster writes in *The Inimitable Jeeves*:

> I wouldn't have said off-hand that there was anything particularly fascinating about me - in fact, most people look upon me as rather an ass.

Wodehouse's great love was writing, and his favourite conversational topic was the mechanics and business of writing. Bertie never sought to be the centre of attention, and neither did Wodehouse, who would not set out to light up a room in the manner we envisage Oscar Wilde doing - though Wilde, too, had a reputation as a good and courteous listener. Although Wilde and Wodehouse worked in dissimilar ways, they worked on similar themes. Wilde's finest play, *The Importance of Being Earnest*, opens with Algernon playing the piano badly but enthusiastically and asking of his manservant:

'Did you hear what I was playing, Lane?'
'I didn't think it polite to listen, sir.'

Such dialogue would not be out of place in a Wooster-Jeeves conversation. Nor would the scene where Algernon, having scoffed all the sandwiches specifically requested by his guests before they arrive, picks up an empty plate in horror when he comes to offer them around:

'Good heavens! Lane! Why are there no cucumber sandwiches? I ordered them specifically.'
'There were no cucumbers in the market this morning, sir. I went down twice.'
'No cucumbers!'
'No, sir. Not even for ready money.'

It is in this play that Miss Prism tells Cecily to 'read your Political Economy in my absence. The chapter on the Fall of the Rupee you may omit. It is somewhat too sensational for a young girl. Even these metallic problems have their melodramatic side.' Wodehouse blamed the fall of the rupee on his not going to university:

My father, after many years in Hong Kong, had retired on a pension, and the authorities paid it to him in rupees. A thoroughly dirty trick, in my opinion, for the rupee is the last thing in the world

- or was then - with anyone who valued his peace of mind would wish to be associated. It never stayed put for a second. It was always jumping up and down and throwing fits, and expenditure had to be regulated in the light of what mood it happened to be at the moment. 'Watch that rupee!' was the cry in the Wodehouse family. [*Over Seventy*]

Take any book of quotations and not only should it be stuffed full of Wodehouse quotes if it is any good, but the majority will be from the Wooster stories. It is Bertie who writes: 'He spoke with a certain what-is-it in his voice, and I could see that while not exactly disgruntled, he was far from feeling gruntled' [*The Code Of The Woosters*] and: 'she fitted into my best armchair as if it had been built round her by someone who knew that they were wearing armchairs tight round the hips this season.' [*Jeeves And The Unbidden Guest*] The Wooster stories were the best work that Wodehouse the craftsman produced, the flagship, as it were, of his writing. He was aware of this:

Do you find you write more slowly than you used to? I don't know if it is because *The Mating Season* is a Jeeves story, and in a Jeeves story every line has to have some entertainment value, but I consider it a good day's work if I can get three pages done. [*Performing Flea*]

That the stories are written in the first person is a handicap and a strength. The handicap is that nothing can happen for the reader unless Bertie sees or hears it - hence the reason he is always having to dive behind sofas - or gets told about it. They require that the reader must be able to understand Jeeves' motives and intentions, while Bertie cannot, and that the conduit for us to comprehend Jeeves is Bertie himself. He must tell the reader what he himself does not know. In doing this so well, Wodehouse displays his genius. He is a far more subtle writer than his detractors have acknowledged.

One of the strengths of Wooster as a participant is that the action in his stories start very promptly. In some of his novels Wodehouse talks a leisurely stroll around the central characters, gently setting the scene and drawing together the various strands from which the plot will be launched, and the main action of the novel may only start a third of the way in. Bertie is always only a few pages away from imminent disaster wherever you might be in the book.

Though Wodehouse often writes in the first person, the Wooster tales are unusual in that the narrator is also a participant. The Ukridge stories are in the first person, but of a minor character, who has little action; indeed, it would not be remotely difficult to rewrite the Ukridge stories in the third person. The Mulliner tales are told by a non-combatant narrator. This device allows Wodehouse to unleash some fairly unlikely plot lines, on the excuse that they are the tall stories of a pub bore. Perhaps 'bore' is not the *mot juste*, but Wodehouse, in a letter to William Townend about correcting the proofs of the Mulliner omnibus wrote: 'It humbled me a good deal, as the stuff didn't seem that good. Still, I suppose nothing would, if you read 864 pages of it straight off.' [*Performing Flea*] It is no coincidence that the name of the public house Mulliner tells his tales in is the Angler's Rest. The first person Oldest Member stories also allow a certain licence with credibility. Wooster is also an exceptional Wodehouse narrator in that he is a comic narrator, the humour of his stories coming as much from how he says things as the action he describes.

Jeeves and Wooster started in short stories, the medium where their relationship works best. The best Jeeves book is *The Inimitable Jeeves*, the first one devoted solely to Jeeves and Wooster. It is a novel crafted from ten short stories, and thus combines the best of both worlds. There is a coherent narrative plot spreading from story to story and Jeeves has a major role to play throughout the book. Wodehouse followed this with two short story collections, *Carry On, Jeeves*, (which reprinted the four Jeeves stories from *My Man Jeeves*) and *Very Good, Jeeves*. The standard of these fail to match the consistent excellence of the stories of *The Inimitable Jeeves*. After that, Wooster and Jeeves were almost solely limited to novels.

When Wodehouse moved over to writing pure novels Jeeves dropped out of the picture rather, and the balance between Wooster and Jeeves was skewed. Jeeves cannot be on hand to provide succour. If he were, the book is in danger of ending dozens of pages too early. So Bertie labours on alone for much of the action. Indeed, in some of the later novels Jeeves hardly has a chance to plot away - or even direct strategy. Whereas in the earlier stories Jeeves was earning Bertie's forfeits of purple socks or whatever, by the end of the chronicles Bertie is offering them up, perhaps for old times' sake and to hide from the reader that Jeeves has really only been a bit-part player in the major action.

In *Jeeves And The Feudal Spirit* Jeeves does not contribute any schemes to save Bertie, nor is he ever called upon to do so. Jeeves does not even extract Bertie from his engagement to Florence Craye. This happens through the revelation that Percy Gorringe pawned his mother's necklace purely so he can put on his dramatisation of Florence Craye's *Spindrift*, which causes Florence to decide her future lies with this devoted admirer instead. Jeeves' involvement is little more than being the one possessed of the knowledge of pearls required to unmask Ma Trotter's necklace as a copy, and the one who provides the pick-me-up which restores LG Trotter's happiness and leads him to take Milady's Boudoir off Aunt Dahlia's hands. This pick-me-up business is not a particularly credible piece of plotting and seems bunged in to try to justify Jeeves' presence in the book. Jeeves could almost as easily, as far as the plot is concerned, have taken the book off. Indeed, he takes part of it off, returning to London to chair the monthly meeting of the Junior Ganymede.

The norm is for Jeeves to be kept out of great chunks of 'his' novels. In *Jeeves In The Offing*, he is off on his annual holiday, from which Bertie recalls him halfway through the book. In *Aunts Aren't Gentlemen* he goes away to visit his aunt. In *Joy In The Morning*, Lord Worplesdon commandeers his services and makes him stay with him. In *The Mating Season*, Bertie is pretending to be Gussie, so Jeeves cannot make an appearance until Gussie arrives pretending to be Bertie, with Bertie's manservant in tow, and even when he does, he departs again for London to attend a lecture. In *Thank You, Jeeves*, Jeeves departs from Bertie's employment in the first chapter, and only rejoins it in the final one.

In *The Code Of The Woosters*, considered by many to be the best of the Wooster novels, Jeeves has little part in the plot, offering only suggestions or information about Spode's 'Eulalie' rather than be allowed to run free to work his machinations. The book is excellent, and has both pace and a convoluted, smooth plot; but it is not one which would be chosen by Jeeves' public relations advisors as an example of what he is capable of.

In the novels, Bertie Wooster was reverting towards being a Reggie Pepper figure.

Knight Draws In

The Wodehouses left France for America on 18 April 1947. The American authorities had studied the Cussen Report into his wartime 'guilt' before they had granted him a visa. Wodehouse gave a press conference on his arrival, arranged by his US publishers to publicise his new novel *Full Moon*. This was one of the novels he had written during the war. At Le Touquet, when he had been taken prisoner, he had been working on *Joy In The Morning*, and when Ethel joined him in Berlin after his release from camp, she brought the manuscript with her, and he finished it in Germany. *Money In The Bank* had been written in captivity and had been serialised in the *Saturday Evening Post* and then published as a book in America in January 1942. During the war *Eggs, Beans And Crumpets* had been published in Britain in April 1940 and in America a month later, and *Quick Service* had come out in October of that year, with the American edition appearing a month later.

Wodehouse had wanted that his book of his wartime experiences, provisionally entitled Wodehouse In Wonderland, be published soon after the war. However his agent in England and his publishers on both sides of the Atlantic fought shy of the idea. They wanted a policy of business as usual, with little reference being made to his wartime activities, and that the first post-war publication from Wodehouse be a novel. They wanted no reminders about his wartime broadcasts.

Whether Wodehouse was right to go along with this has been questioned. Many have argued that he should have taken on his accusers head on and dealt with the charges made against him. Instead a policy of ignoring them and trying to re-establish 'normality' in the 'Wodehouse brand', was decided upon. This might have served his publishers' interests more than his own. Contrary to his publishers' advice, Wodehouse sought to give his side of the argument for his wartime broadcasts in an interview to Hubert Cole of the British magazine *Illustrated*, which appeared in the issue of 7 December 1946, and in a letter to the Chairman of the Old Alleyians, extracts of which were published in *The Alleyian* of July 1945, and a letter to *Variety*, which was published on 8 May 1946.

Wodehouse could have been more insistent on trying to clear his name. But it is hard to be critical of a man who had suffered great deprivation both emotionally and physically during the war years. He had lost three stones in weight, had suffered the death of his beloved step-daughter, been denounced as a traitor in Parliament and seen old friends turn on him and the press publish repeated falsehoods about him. He was battered and bruised and one can sympathise if he did not have the fight in him to continue to take on the perceived wisdom ranged against him.

In time, he came to hate talk of his wartime broadcasts. He had intended to publish a version of these talks in *Performing Flea*, which came out in 1953. He re-read the broadcasts he had made and was upset to find that he had talked of 'fraternising' with the Germans and 'beaming'; in addition there was the passage where he criticised the Belgians, allies of the British. He also felt that the talks' humour could be improved, as he had originally rushed through the texts and had not had time to polish them. However, his publishers would only publish the texts as he had actually spoken them, and so Wodehouse decided not to publish the broadcasts in *Performing Flea*, partly because he feared they would be misunderstood, and also because of professional pride as he judged them an inferior piece of work. He later published the new, improved version of the broadcasts in *Encounter* in late 1954. The manuscript of Wodehouse In Wonderland is believed to have been deliberately destroyed, though when is not clear. When Richard Usborne planned to publish *Wodehouse At Work*, which had been commissioned by Wodehouse's publishers, with a chapter on Wodehouse's wartime activities, Wodehouse ensured that no such chapter appeared.

The first Wodehouse work to be published in Britain after the war was *Money In the Bank*. It sold 26,000 copies in the first month. 450,000 copies of Wodehouse's works had been sold between 1941 and the end of the war which showed that some of his public were prepared to stand by him, either not judging him guilty of being a traitor, or able to separate the work from the man. However Wodehouse was sufficiently uncertain of his reputation in the land of his birth that when his collaboration with Guy Bolton *Don't Listen, Ladies* was put on in London the playwrights were billed as Guy Bolton and Stephen Powys. Ethel visited England to see the production, but Wodehouse was unable to. It was only in the 1960s that he was unofficially assured that it would be safe for him to return to Britain free of potential arrest. By then, in his eighties, he had ceased to travel out of the country or, indeed, much out of the village he lived in.

Public opinion towards Wodehouse gradually became less hostile. When he returned to America the *Saturday Evening Post* refused to look at his work and the BBC were still continuing with their policy of banning his works. But in 1950 the BBC asked for permission to broadcast a dramatisation of *A Damsel In Distress*. Further acceptance back into the British literary world occurred when Wodehouse's friend Malcolm Muggeridge took over the editorship of *Punch* and asked Wodehouse to write a regular column. In 1953 a further sign of re-acceptance came when Penguin published five of his back catalogue simultaneously: *The Inimitable Jeeves*; *Leave It To Psmith*; *Big Money*; *Right Ho, Jeeves* and *The Code of The Woosters*.

Just as Muggeridge, who had first met Wodehouse during the war when as a member of military intelligence he had investigated the author, remembered his friend, so too did Wodehouse remember those who stood by him, and those who did not. One of those who did was Arthur Thompson, a solicitors' clerk whom he had met in 1913. Though they hardly saw each other from then on, their friendship continued by post for over 40 years. During the war Thompson was an active defender of Wodehouse and wrote to local papers in areas where councils had banned Wodehouse's books. Wodehouse gave him the script of, and production rights to, *Joy In The Morning*. This was originally called *Phipps* and is the play from which *The Old Reliable* was written, and has no connection with the Jeeves and Wooster novel of the same name - Wodehouse's recycling did not just extend to plots, but titles as well. This play had never been performed, and so the world premiere took place in Ashburton in Devon, performed by the amateur group the Buckfast Players.

Others were not remembered so fondly, and Wodehouse took the chance to have a mild revenge in *The Mating Season*. Gussie Fink-Nottle is arrested for going newt hunting in a fountain in Trafalgar Square and 'showing unexpected intelligence, gave his name as Alfred Duff Cooper.' Another passing swipe is made at another of his wartime critics, the Old Alleyian Eustace Pulbrook, when Eustacia Pulbrook gives a violin recital which 'had that quality that which I have noticed in all violin solos, of seeming to last much longer than it did.'

But the person most in Wodehouse's sights was AA Milne. Milne and Wodehouse had been friends, and Milne had been one of the backers of one of Wodehouse's plays. But during the war Milne had turned on Wodehouse and wrote to *The Daily Telegraph* that:

> I remember he told me once he wished he had a son; and he added characteristically (and quite sincerely):

'But he would have to be born at the age of 15, when he was just getting into his House eleven.' You see the advantage of that. Bringing up a son throws a considerable responsibility on a man; but by the time the boy is 15 one has shifted the responsibility onto the housemaster.'

Wodehouse was angered by this attack from someone he had considered a friend, if not a close one. Moreover Milne had taken a comment by one of Wodehouse's characters, Mike, and made it out to be Wodehouse's view instead. Milne's exploitation of his own family was sent up in the golfing story *Rodney Has A Relapse*, in which Rodney Spelvin gives up writing detective fiction to write poems about his young son, which he hopes to publish in a slim volume. In one of the draft poems he describes his son as going 'hoppity hoppity hop'. Rodney's brother-in-law, William, does not approve:

'What it comes to,' said William, 'is that he is wantonly laying up a lifetime of shame and misery for the wretched little moppet. In the years to come, when he is playing in the National Amateur, the papers will print photographs of him with captions underneath explaining that he is the Timothy Bobbin of the well-known poems -'

In *The Mating Season*, soppy Madeline Bassett wants Gussie to recite at the local concert. Bertie is pretending to be Gussie, with whom he is talking:

'Those Christopher Robin poems. Here they are.'
He handed me a slim volume of verses and I gave it the perplexed eye.
'What's this for?'
'You recite them at the concert. The ones marked with a cross. I was to have recited them, Madeline

making a great point of it - you know how fond she is of the Christopher Robin poems - but now, of course, we have switched acts. And I don't mind telling you that I feel extremely relieved. There's one about the little blighter going hoppity-hoppity-hop which... well, as I say, I feel extremely relieved.'

The slim volume slipped from my nerveless fingers, and I goggled at him.

'But dash it!'

'It's no good saying "But dash, it!" Do you think that I didn't say "But, dash it!" when she forced these nauseous productions on me? You've got to do them. She insists. The first thing she will want to know is how they went.'

'But the tough eggs at the back of the row will rush the stage and lynch me.'

'I shouldn't wonder.'

And later, Wodehouse twists the knife a little further:

I was sorry for the unhappy young blister of course, but it piqued me somewhat that he seemed to consider that he was the only one who had any troubles.

'Well, I've got Christopher Robin poems.'

'Pah!' he said. 'It might have been Winnie The Pooh.'

Well, there was that, of course.

Wodehouse again returned to the subject of Alfred Duff Cooper in *Cocktail Time*, which concerns a would-be politician who has written a sensational book. Cooper had written a biography of Earl Haig and another on Tallyrand:

Literary composition is not entirely barred to those whose ambition it is to carve for themselves a political career, but it has to be the right sort of literary composition - a scholarly life of Tallyrand for instance.

As well as containing digs at some of those whose conduct Wodehouse had taken exception to, some of his post-war works can be seen to be influenced by his wartime experiences in other ways. In *Joy In The Morning*, Wodehouse is at great pains to point out that writers can suffer from a lack of common sense:

> One has of course to make allowances for writers, all of them being more or less potty.
> I doubt you can ever trust an author not to make an ass of himself.
> I am not a vindictive man, but I was feeling in no amiable frame of mind towards this literary screwball. I mean, it's all very well for a chap to plead he's an author and expect on the strength of it to get away with conduct which would qualify the ordinary man for a one-way ticket to Colney Hatch.

One of Wodehouse's defences of his wartime conduct was to ask for forgiveness and understanding as he realised that he had been 'an ass'. These passages from *Joy In The Morning*, which was published in 1946 in America and a year later in Britain, can be seen a furtherance of this aim. But Wodehouse was not down on his profession of authorship far from it. His dislike of politicians, and side-swipes at them, had been a feature of his pre-war work. Now they often took a different style, in that politicians were compared unfavourably with authors. In *Joy In The Morning* comes this aside:

> You can't get away from it that he is one of the hottest of England's young litterateurs. He earns more per annum than a Cabinet Minister.

In *Much Obliged, Jeeves*, Bertie Wooster gives up canvassing for his friend Ginger Winship and retires from the political fight for a fight over a Rex Stout novel. *Much Obliged, Jeeves* is critical of politics. Bertie Wooster is campaigning for a friend just because he is a pal as he has little understanding of the policies or issues involved. The candidate, Ginger Winship, is prepared to lose the election because love is more important than politics. Spode's interest in getting into the House of Commons is depicted to be shallow when he abandons the idea after a potato is thrown at him at a political rally. Spode is never shown as possessing a desire to create a better world by his presence in the Commons, he is merely concerned in finding a suitable platform for his oratory.

Cocktail Time also brings the world of politics and literature into competition, and Sir Raymond Bastable chooses the world of literature. Lord Ickenham gives him this advice about the lower house:

> 'Well, why do you want a political career? Have you ever been in the House of Commons and taken a good square look at the inmates? As weird a gaggle of freaks and sub-humans as was ever collected in one spot. I wouldn't mix with them for any money you could offer me.'

Wodehouse was to continue to cheer himself up with a few sideswipes at politicians in the Wooster novels:

> I love Gus like a brother, but after years of non-stop sleep he has about as much genuine intelligence as a Cabinet minister. [*Much Obliged, Jeeves*]
> I knew the old relative to be quite choosy in the matter of guests. Cabinet ministers have sometimes failed to crash the gate. [*Jeeves And The Feudal Spirit*]
> I had always supposed that poachers were tough-looking eggs who wore whatever they could borrow

from the nearest scarecrow and shaved only once a week. He, to the contrary, was neatly clad in form-fitting tweeds and was shaven to the bone. His eyes were frank and blue, his hair a becoming grey. I have seen more raffish cabinet ministers. [*Aunts Aren't Gentlemen*]

One of the more surprising reverberations of the wartime controversy was sparked off again by the publication of *Performing Flea*, a heavily edited selection of letters from Wodehouse to Townend. The book was carefully proof-read by libel lawyers, who suggested deleting the phrase 'lawyers really are the damnedest fools.' From this book sprang events which led to the forming of a friendship between Wodehouse and William Connor, of the infamous Cassandra broadcasts. In *Performing Flea*, Wodehouse had remembered that Cassandra had accused him of being called Pelham Grenville and hoped that the WD in WD Connor stood for Walpurgis Diarmid. Connor took up the theme in a *Daily Mirror* article - pointing out, among other things, that his initials were actually WN - and a lunch was arranged between the two of them. Out of this grew a friendship, and they would lunch together when Connor came to New York and kept up a regular correspondence. Wodehouse's letters were always addressed 'Dear Walp'.

This friendship has puzzled many. Was Wodehouse really so saintly that he could forgive someone who had damaged him so greatly? It is possible. It is also a possibility that he recognised that, if his greatest wartime accuser was going round saying that Wodehouse was actually a great bloke and a good pal of his, then this would be very beneficial to his reputation and Wodehouse might have set out for that initial lunch determined to become friends.

As Wodehouse got older his output slowed down. He spent less time each day writing, and when he worked he frequently found he was not able to rattle through the work as quickly as he once could. But all things are relative. Between 1946 and 1974 at least one new Wodehouse book was published in Britain each year, with the exception of 1955.

His inspiration was slightly on the wane. His novels became shorter and the process by which he put them together changed. Earlier in his career he had frequently over-written and at the polishing and revision stage he had to prune back his work. By the end of his career he was writing very short, and the polishing stage involved putting a lot of extra material in to plump out the work. This is graphically shown in *Sunset At Blandings*, an unfinished novel Wodehouse was working on at the time of his death. Wodehouse had written the draft copy of 16 chapters of a 22-chapter novel. These amount to only 30,000 words; at that ratio the finished book would only consist of around 40,000 words. Some of his earlier novels are two-and-a-half times this length. The 'industry standard' novel is normally at least 60,000 words. Wodehouse would have gone back through the text adding fresh material as much as revising.

It is a shame in a way that this unfinished novel came to be published, though the editing and notes by Richard Usborne throws light on Wodehouse's methods of construction as well on his working techniques. Artistically, *A Pelican At Blandings* would have been a happier end to the Blandings saga. It has the feel of a retirement book. Lord Emsworth starts the book happy and alone at his castle, believing he is at last free of potential interruptions from his sisters. At the end of the book this happy state is returned to, with Gally and Emsworth unaccompanied at the castle. It would be a suitable drawing down of the curtain on Blandings. Wodehouse, who was 87 when the book was published, might consciously or sub-consciously have conceived it as such.

As Wodehouse got older so, too, did the new characters in his books. The author was in his late forties when he created Gally Threepwood who was only a few years his senior. His later works outside the Jeeves and Blandings cycles feature romances between the older generation and *Sunset At Blandings* features such a romance at its core.

When the Wodehouses first returned to New York they took an apartment in New York City. Guy Bolton had a house in the Long Island settlement of Remsenburg, and the Wodehouses bought a house there, too. Originally this was for use as a summer house, with their New York apartment being their base for the winter months, but in 1955 they gave up the apartment and moved to Remsenburg permanently. They bought the surrounding land to provide privacy. This land included a wood which ran down to a river. Here Wodehouse would exercise the dogs which were a central part of the extended family which also contained a number of cats. Some of these animals had come to the house as strays.

In his essay *In Defence of PG Wodehouse*, George Orwell had written: 'if we drive him to retire to the United States and renounce his British citizenship, we shall end up being horribly ashamed of ourselves.' What Orwell had feared transpired. The British government was still unwilling to forgive Wodehouse and on 16 December 1955 Wodehouse took out American nationality. He gave as his public reasons the fact that it cut back on red tape if he wanted to make a trip out of the country - which he by then had no intention of doing anyway - and that it seemed good manners to be a national of the county one lived in. Wodehouse was to end his life having lived in America for longer than he had in Britain. But he retained his English accent throughout his life, and his manuscripts were written with English spellings. The language he wrote in had always been freely adapted from the slang and idioms of both his native land and his adopted one. Normally he did so unselfconsciously, although sometimes he felt the need to slip footnotes into the text as he went along:

> Coshes they are called, though blackjack is, I believe
> the American term [*Jeeves And The Feudal Spirit*]

Despite settling permanently in America, he would still set most of his work in England, even though, by the time he was writing his final work, he had not set foot in his native land for about forty years, nearly half his lifetime. In his language Wodehouse had carved out a world of his own; it was here that his England was situated. The march of time had only a cursory influence on Wodehouse's fiction and some of his later works are hard to pin down to any set period. *The Code of the Woosters*, by nature of Spode's dictatorship, is obviously set in the 1930s, the decade in which it was written. *Jeeves In The Offing* must be set no earlier than the 1960s as Spode is threatening to revoke his peerage, something which it only became possible do to by an Act of Parliament early in this decade. However the characters are not thirty years older than they were in *The Code of the Woosters* and Bertie is still happily going to stay at country houses with his valet in tow without it being remarkable - which, by the 1960s it would most certainly have been. Victory in the parliamentary by-election is between the Liberal and Conservative parties and there does not appear to be a Labour candidate. Shortly after when *The Code of the Woosters* was set, England was in a world war, but that is not when *Jeeves In The Offing* takes place. World wars are rarely registered in Wodehouse's work, although Jeeves was involved in the First World War as was the hero of the *Indiscretions Of Archie*, and Lord Ickenham and Peasemarch were both in the Home Guard in the Second World War.

Perhaps Wodehouse's work can be best termed as increasingly anachronistic, or maybe it is simply that it became even less anchored in any particular period of English history. He had created his template for his characters to work in, and this remained virtually constant throughout, with a few minor modifications and updates when the plot required it. Thus in *Cocktail Time*, Lord Ickenham is watching television in a pub, but he is doing so only so that it can give him an idea of how to hide a letter. Sometimes Wodehouse would be aware that his plots belonged to an age since past, and would excuse them. Even during the war he was writing this in *Joy In the Morning*:

> If I were to submit a story to your aunt about a girl who couldn't marry a fellow without some blasted head of family's consent, she would hoot at it. That is to say, I am not allowed to turn an honest penny by using this complication in any work, but it is jolly well allowed to come barging in and ruining my life.

After the war he moved away from writing short stories. Only three of his 32 post-war works are collections of short stories; whereas he published thirteen collections before the war and two of his novels, *The Inimitable Jeeves* and *Indiscretions Of Archie*, started life as a series of magazine short stories. This reflected market conditions: there was no longer a plethora of magazines around which published short stories, so Wodehouse rarely wrote them. One magazine which did publish short stories was *Playboy*, so Wodehouse wrote for that, and these stories found their way into *A Few Quick Ones* and *Plum Pie*. *Playboy* also serialised *Frozen Assets*.

Wodehouse became more reclusive as he got older. He rarely travelled from Remsenburg, and grew to love the solitude and privacy of the area. It was a place where it was possible to walk around without seeing a soul, apart from a gardener or two. This was more Plum's idea of bliss than Ethel's, who was always naturally sociable, whereas her husband's degree of reserve and shyness meant he was always politely sociable. Wodehouse, however, was not the total recluse some have painted him as. Journalists came to the house to interview him. He would go for walks with Guy Bolton when Bolton was around and he would travel to New York to preside at dinners of a branch of the Old Alleyian Society or to have lunch with English friends who were over in America. The Old Alleyian dinners were changed to Sunday lunches so that Wodehouse would not have to spend a night away from Remsenburg. His daily pattern was to do his exercises before breakfast which had been a feature of his life since 1919, and were based upon an article he had read in *Collier's*. His exercising would occupy three-quarters of an hour, after which he would make his own breakfast. After breakfast he would settle down to work until midday whereupon he would watch television until lunch. After lunch he would take the dogs for a walk to collect the post. He might return to do some more work, before having a bath round five o'clock prior to cocktails and the evening meal. The Wodehouses ate early so as to allow their maid, who did not live in, to return home in good time. After dinner he would sometimes play two-handed bridge with Ethel or he would read. In 1964 Armine's widow, Nella, came to live with them.

His health deteriorated as he aged. He had a giddy fit while out walking, and managed to totter into a doctor's surgery. The doctor thought that a 'bum' had stumbled in who was either seriously ill or very drunk. He called for an ambulance to take him to Bellevue Hospital where derelicts were normally sent. In an effort to discover his unexpected patient's identity, he went through his pockets and discovered that the well-loved jacket had been made in Savile Row, the scruffy shoes were of a good make and that the visitor's fingernails were manicured. The ambulance was directed to an upmarket private hospital instead. As well as having a stroke in his seventies, Wodehouse was later diagnosed as having a brain tumour. He faced up to what he supposed would be the end of him, as he felt he was unable to survive an operation at his age. This diagnosis was later changed to one of 'don't know' and he was to live for another twenty-two years. By the end of his life arthritis meant that he could only get around with some difficulty with a walking stick. Ethel was often confined to bed by ill health, yet she was to outlive her husband by nine years.

In November 1974 Wodehouse received a telephone call from the British Consul General in Washington asking him whether he would accept a knighthood if one were offered.

This was a question demanded by protocol, rather than by a worry that Wodehouse might snub Britain after his wartime treatment. Wodehouse duly received a knighthood in the New Year's Honours of 1975. Another knighted in this list was the 87-year old Charlie Chaplin, Wodehouse's junior by half a dozen years. Wodehouse was too old to travel to Britain for the ceremony, but the Queen Mother, a keen reader of Wodehouse, was eager to travel to America to present him with his gong; as she later telegraphed to the Wodehouse centenary celebrations in New York, she was 'a devoted admirer of his work'. But her schedules could not be re-arranged to allow this, so it was arranged that the ceremony would be held in the British Consulate at New York with the British Ambassador coming from Washington to confer the award.

But, before then, Wodehouse went into hospital suffering from pemphiguf, a skin disorder. He took with him the manuscript of the novel he was engaged upon and a song lyric he was working on. He had continued to work on song lyrics even though he had long since stopped working in musical theatre. On Valentine's Day he got out of bed to walk across the room, and died. The Remsenburg post office lowered its flag to half mast, where it hung just clear of the piled-up snow. A fortnight later the Acting Consul General drove out from New York and presented Wodehouse's insignia and warrant to Lady Wodehouse.

Timeless

Will there ever be another like PG Wodehouse? Indeed, how could there be another like him? He was a product of his age, and the conditions which forged him as a writer are no longer present in contemporary society.

His career depended upon two foundations. The principle one was the proliferation of magazines which published fiction around the time he became a freelancer. Indeed, it was only because of this that he was able to set out on the freelance path. What would a banking clerk do now if he wanted to become a fiction writer? What they could not do is chuck in their day job confident in the knowledge of selling enough pieces to magazines to make a living while they honed their craft. Few magazines these days publish fiction, and those that do tend to hunt out the stories they publish from established names. Wodehouse was in the right place at the right time. The Victorian love of reading, universal education and the absence of many competing attractions led to a healthy market for budding writers. Often a story of his would do the rounds of the magazines before it was accepted, and the Wodehouse bank account had a further addition. Some of his work he did not manage to sell to anyone.

> Never give in. Perseverance brings home the gravy. If you get an article accepted, send another article to that editor. If you get an article refused, send that

article to another editor. [*The Inferiority Complex of Old Sippy*]

Wodehouse received an on-the-job training in his chosen profession. He could devote all his time to his craft as it was self-funding. He needed this period in his life for he had to serve a reasonably long apprenticeship before he hit his stride. His near contemporary and correspondent - they met only once - Evelyn Waugh had *Decline And Fall* published while he was still in his mid- twenties, which many consider to be his best work, although *The Loved One* has a better claim to that honour. *Decline And Fall* was Waugh's first novel. In comparison, Psmith first appeared in Wodehouse's eleventh book of fiction. Many literary reputations have been based on a career total of fewer than eleven books. Three Bronte sisters built their reputation on a combined total of five novels. Anne's and Emily's were published when they were in their twenties.

The second aspect of Wodehouse's early life which had a strong influence on his career was his thorough grounding in the classics and that he was widely read. When he was growing up there were fewer distractions for youngsters, particularly as there was no television. Later in life he was to grumble at the difficulty of finding something good to read which he had not already read. By now, too, he had the competing distraction of television, and became hooked on soap operas. When he wondered where the good modern writers were as they did not seem to be producing novels for him to read, he decided that they must be working in television instead. (In this would only be following a career pattern similar to Wodehouse's, for when he became established as a writer he went to work for the recorded visual medium when he set out for Hollywood.) One of the most successful of modern British comedy films, *Four Weddings And A Funeral*, uses a template Wodehouse would have recognised: upper-class English settings - which include a castle - and a love affair between an American and a traditional, tongue-tied English gentleman. One of the most brilliant of television situation comedies, *Yes Minister*, has, in the two central roles, characters whose relationship is very much a Bertie/Jeeves one. The minister, Jim Hacker, is well-meaning but frequently ineffectual; his civil servant, Sir Humphrey, is reactionary and manipulates situations to his own ends, while pretending to serve faithfully his political master, for whom he has little respect. Sir Humphrey is also keen at one stage to retain Hacker as his employer as he has him nicely 'house-trained' to use his own phrase.

Wodehouse's breadth of reading fed through to his writing, not only by giving him ideas for plots and characters but in the way that he frequently, and deliberately, adapts quotations from others' work. Bertie Wooster is particularly fascinated by great literature and encourages Jeeves' love of direct quotation, but there are many phrases and sayings which find their way unannounced into his work. One of Wodehouse's favourite sources is Shakespeare, particularly in his work during, and after, the Second World War, as he took with him the complete works into internment. The description, from *The Merchant Of Venice*, of the stars 'still quiring to the young-eyed Cherubim' finds its way into both *The Mating Season* and *Joy In The Morning*, although in both cases Wodehouse/Wooster prefers not to age the Cherubim. Wodehouse would tend to quote from memory, and so it is not always clear whether he is adapting or simply misquoting. In the same play Balthazar tells Portia that he goes with 'all convenient speed' which is how Bertie urges Jeeves to act in *Jeeves And The Yuletide Spirit*.

For someone who borrowed and adapted so freely from others, it shows a degree of opportunism to set his lawyer onto Eric Hodgins for writing a work just after the Second World War entitled *Mr Blandings Builds His Castle,* subsequently to become *Mr Blandings Builds His Dream House*. Wodehouse was awarded $1,500 for the plagiarism.

The modern author, I told him, is keen and hard-hearted. He is out for the stuff, and when he gets it he salts it away. [*Joy In The Morning*]

In adapting quotations or well-known sayings Wodehouse was only doing what legions of sub-editors do when looking for a headline. Indeed, Kipling's comment that 'a woman is only a woman, but a good cigar is a smoke' [*The Betrothed*] split into two gave Wodehouse the titles for two of his short stories, the first appearing in 1919, the second in 1967.

In this respect, Wodehouse's work does age, for his references will not necessarily be picked up by a later generation. He talks about people whose names many modern readers will not recognise. His formal school education was in the 19th century, and tastes in literature have moved on. But in other respects his work is timeless. It deals with universal themes such as love; reputation and social standing; manipulation and the difference between perspective and reality. His work will age less than that of others writing at the same time because of the way he carved out his own distinct writing style and language, and that his work is not really rooted in any particular moment in history. It has a loose anchor in the Edwardian period, but this mooring becomes extremely loose at times in his later work. The great adapter had taken a time and place - Edwardian England - and fashioned his own distinct series of takes upon it. Only rarely, such as in *The Code Of The Woosters*, do events of the world in which Wodehouse was living imprint itself firmly on the narrative of his work.

Wodehouse was always fascinated by language. What many detractors fail to acknowledge is that he was, at his best, a superb writer of English. His sentences are beautifully balanced and, in an age when punctuation often seems an optional extra, many could learn from reading Wodehouse. In making notes for this book I would frequently scribble down quotes or passages from Wodehouse's work. Often these would be done at speed and often I had already written down the word I expected to come next; on inspection, I frequently found that Wodehouse had used a different one. On every occasion this had markedly improved the sentence. That one word could make such a difference was a great personal revelation regarding his craft as a writer. At his best, Wodehouse made the English language dance.

The *Oxford English Dictionary* cites Wodehouse 192 times as the inventor or first recorded user of a phrase or particular use of a word in a specific sense or with a certain nuance. How many of these were Wodehouse inventions, rather than the result of his happening to pick up on something and being the first known to use it, is not clear. Wodehouse had a good ear for language. Some phrases Wodehouse used were clearly taken from other fields. For instance he is credited with the first citing of 'one up' (1923; *Leave It To Psmith*), meaning to be ahead; this surely comes from matchplay golf. Similarly, 'non-starter' (1934; *Right Ho, Jeeves*) to mean an unimpressive person, is a phrase taken from the racing world.

The total undoubtedly flatters Wodehouse's powers of invention. The editors themselves admit that he is only the first user that they have discovered. But it is interesting that he is suggested as the inventor of such phrases as 'down to earth', 'pain in the neck' and 'loony bin'.

Tom Sharpe, a writer whose love, and use, of language means that his novels have more in common with Wodehouse's than a superficial comparison of their subject matter might suggest, was an admirer of Wodehouse's work. Evelyn Waugh said that 'one has to regard a man as a Master who can produce on average three uniquely brilliant and entirely original similes to every page.' Hilaire Belloc described him as 'the best writer of English now alive'. As a craftsman of the English language Wodehouse was much admired by his writing peers.

The sheer number of Wodehouse novels and short-story collections can trap the newcomer. If someone, tempted to try his work through his reputation, selected a book at random and it was, for example, the short story collection *The Man With Two Left Feet*, they would be surprised at the reputation the writer had garnered. Not least because two of the stories deal with planned suicides. They would also be puzzled at finding a Bertie story in which Jeeves has only a two-line part and serves a master who is called Mannering-Phipps. If they persevered and decided to give this author another try and happened to pick, say, *The Coming Of Bill*, then they undoubtedly would not come back for more. Yet if the lucky dip from the library shelves happened to alight upon, say, *Heavy Weather* or *The Code of The Woosters* then that reader is more likely to understand what all the fuss is about.

Part of the reason for the variation in quality of the output is due to the fact that Wodehouse wrote for 72 years yet, unsurprisingly, was not at his peak for all of this time. It is often stated that Wodehouse was at his zenith in the years immediately before the Second World War or perhaps, more expansively, throughout the thirties, his fifties. The last three books he published prior to the war were *Summer Moonshine*, *The Code of the Woosters* and *Uncle Fred In The Springtime*. He brought out 17 books during this decade, one less than the figure for the previous one.

Yet although Wodehouse's output fluctuated in quality, his best work does not fit neatly into any time period. Compiling a top ten of Wodehouse's novels is a highly subjective exercise. But there are books from various stages of his writing career which would deserve serious consideration. The opening decade of the 20th century brings *Mike*, the 1910s saw the publication of *Psmith In The City* and *A Damsel In Distress* and the twenties could be represented by *The Inimitable Jeeves* and *Summer Lightning*; the thirties by *Heavy Weather*, *Right Ho, Jeeves* and *The Code of The Woosters*. *Summer Moonshine* was also published in this decade, and it must lay a strong claim to be the best of the novels that are not part of the Blandings/Belpher or Wooster/Jeeves series. Between the publication of *Mike* and *The Code of The Woosters* lies 29 years.

What post-war novels might make a shortlist for a top ten is more obscure, mainly because opinions concerning works from this period seem to vary far more amongst Wodehouse fans, especially in regard to work published from the sixties onwards. It is generally accepted that his products towards the end of his life was not amongst his greatest, although even here there will be dissenting voices. But where the main dissent appears is over what books demonstrate this trend, and which buck it. *Company For Henry* is generally cited as a poor book, but is one I particularly enjoyed, while I have read incredulously that *French Leave* deserves to rank alongside his best works, whereas I found this particular novel tedious. Each to his own.

When someone writes 75 completed novels, and around 300 short stories - some of which were never collected into book form - one can expect a variation in quality. Also, one can excuse the frequent criticism that Wodehouse writes the same book over and over again. In terms of plot, recycling is perhaps unavoidable when one considers such a vast output; just how many radically different plots are there? Indeed, do we not want some similarity in plotting - do we not desire that the boy gets the girl in the end?

This criticism has also been applied to the style of Wodehouse's work. He created his own world and use of language and mined it effectively. No-one does what Wodehouse does nearly so well. So let Wodehouse write what he is good at and let others write what they are good at. I am not going to criticise Wodehouse for not writing books about the problems of being a one-parent family. If I wanted that, I would go to a writer who catered for this. I would not have wanted Wodehouse wasting his time trying to turn out that sort of work, for that is not where his strengths lay. As he himself said: 'I hardly think it would be an improvement if I were to write a novel laid in Yugoslavia or the Crimea.' This is merely a literary application of the economist's comparative advantage theory whereby each society provides the goods which it is good at, leaving other societies to provide the goods which they are best at producing. These societies then trade for the betterment of the world as a whole.

For someone who was so adept, and at ease, with words, it is curious that Wodehouse took so long to get up to form and that there were aspects of writing at which he did not excel. Maybe non-fiction humour dates quicker, but his work in this field is not particularly interesting, nor often even particularly good. The title of the collection *Louder And Funnier* refers to the standard comment from someone at the back of the hall that could the speaker could be a bit louder. A few minutes later he pipes up again: '... and funnier.' The same sadly, could be said of this particular Wodehouse effort. Wodehouse himself said that the best thing about the book was the cover, a drawing by Rex Whistler. With his non-fiction work Wodehouse often is seen to be straining too hard to be funny. Although he could occasionally be sharp, his non-fiction writing either needed to have more of an edge to be a success or he needed to surrender himself more to the whimsical. There is never in his articles an argument which he is trying to put across, and he struggles to make his pieces work without one. An argument could have supplied the plot, and he was always very conscious of the need to get his plot straight and tight before embarking on his fiction. As he showed, this reliance on the plot was necessary. When he wrote non fiction without one he gave no idea of the heights of humour and invention which his writing could attain.

Wodehouse began his career as a hack, turning out whatever he could as often as he could, to turn a penny. When he had established himself he had no need to do this, but the habit died hard. His reputation is slightly dented as a result. Also, his love of writing meant that he always had to have something on the go, and this did sometimes impair the quality of his work. He confessed that *The Old Reliable* was a poorer work than it should have been simply because he did not have enough time to work on it, and so its theatrical roots stand out too starkly.

But Wodehouse below his best underlines quite how monumental are the heights which he could attain. If penetrating insights into the meaning of life and in-depth studies of the human condition are your taste in literature, then Wodehouse is not your man. Nor would he want to be. Those who dislike him because he would write about the idle rich and the aristocracy are making a political complaint not a literary one. The complaint is of doubtful worth in the first place, and is certainly not relevant to his allure as a literary craftsman.

His appeal will be timeless so long as the English language seduces people, and so long as people want to be entertained and escape from some of the tedium and anxiety that life can throw up. He produces, above all, great escapist literature. The broadcaster and humourist Arthur Marshall, at the end of his life, is said to have made a point of reading some PG Wodehouse each night before falling asleep, so that if he died in his sleep he would have done so with a smile on his face.

PG Wodehouse has cheered and amused millions and found great personal fulfilment in doing so. That is not a bad epitaph for anyone.

Appendix

Wodehouse's works of fiction published in Britain in his lifetime

1902 The Pothunters
1903 A Prefect's Uncle; Tales of St Austin's
1904 The Gold Bat; William Tell Told Again
1905 Head of Kay's
1906 Love Among The Chickens (revised edition, 1921)
1907 The White Feather; Not George Washington
1909 The Swoop; Mike
1910 A Gentleman Of Leisure; Psmith In The City
1912 The Prince And Betty
1913 The Little Nugget
1914 The Man Upstairs
1915 Something Fresh; Psmith, Journalist
1917 Uneasy Money; The Man With Two Left Feet
1918 Piccadilly Jim
1919 My Man Jeeves; A Damsel In Distress
1920 The Coming Of Bill
1921 Jill The Reckless; Indiscretions Of Archie
1922 The Clicking Of Cuthbert; The Girl On The Boat; The Adventures Of Sally
1923 The Inimitable Jeeves; Leave It To Psmith
1924 Ukridge; Bill The Conqueror
1925 Carry On, Jeeves; Sam The Sudden
1926 The Heart Of A Goof
1927 The Small Bachelor; Meet Mr Mulliner
1928 Money For Nothing
1929 Mr Mulliner Speaking; Summer Lightning
1930 Very Good, Jeeves
1931 Big Money; If I Were You

1932 Doctor Sally; Hot Water
1933 Heavy Weather
1934 Thank You, Jeeves; Right Ho, Jeeves
1935 Blandings Castle And Elsewhere; The Luck Of The Bodkins
1936 Young Men In Spats; Laughing Gas
1937 Lord Emsworth And Others
1938 Summer Moonshine; The Code Of The Woosters
1939 Uncle Fred In The Springtime
1940 Eggs, Beans And Crumpets; Quick Service
1946 Money In The Bank
1947 Joy In The Morning; Full Moon
1948 Spring Fever; Uncle Dynamite
1949 The Mating Season
1950 Nothing Serious
1951 The Old Reliable
1952 Barmy In Wonderland; Pigs Have Wings
1953 Ring For Jeeves
1954 Jeeves And The Feudal Spirit
1956 French Leave
1957 Something Fishy
1958 Cocktail Time
1959 A Few Quick Ones
1960 Jeeves In The Offing
1961 Ice In The Bedroom
1962 Service With A Smile
1963 Stiff Up Lip, Jeeves
1964 Frozen Assets
1965 Galahad At Blandings
1966 Plum Pie
1967 Company For Henry
1968 Do Butlers Burgle Banks?
1969 A Pelican At Blandings
1970 The Girl In Blue
1971 Much Obliged, Jeeves

1972 Pearls, Girls And Monty Bodkin
1973 Bachelor's Anonymous
1974 Aunts Aren't Gentlemen
1977 Sunset At Blandings (*posthumously*)

Bibliography

After Hours With PG Wodehouse, Richard Usborne
A Wodehouse Companion, Richard Usborne
Beyond The Pale, Nicholas Mosley
Blandings The Blest, Geoffrey Jaggard
Chronicles Of Wasted Time, Malcolm Muggeridge
Cricket Calling, Rowland Ryder
Burkes Peerage and Baronetage
Eight Humorists, George Mikes
In Search Of Blandings, NTP Murphy
Long Before Forty, CS Forester
PG Wodehouse, Frances Donaldson
PG Wodehouse, RBD French
PG Wodehouse: A Critical And Historical Essay,
Owen Dudley Edwards
PG Wodehouse: A Literary Biography, Benny Green
PG Wodehouse: A Portrait Of A Master, David A.
Jasen
PG Wodehouse: Man And Myth, Barry Phelps
Rules Of The Game, Nicholas Mosley
Thank You, Wodehouse, JHC Morris and AD
Maintyre
Who's Who In Wodehouse, Daniel H. Garrison
Wodehouse At The Wicket, edited by Murray
Hedgcock
Wodehouse At War, Iain Sproat
Wodehouse At Work To The End, Richard Usborne
Wodehouse Goes To School, Tony Ring and Geoffrey
Jaggard, with introductory essays by Jan Piggott
Wooster Sauce, the journal of the UK PG Wodehouse
Society, and the society's newsletter *By The Way* and
its website, www.pgwodehousesociety.org.uk, in
particular Information Sheet Number 10.
Wooster's World, Geoffrey Jaggard

Printed in Great Britain
by Amazon